VIKING
AMERICA

VIKING AMERICA

the Norse crossings and their legacy

JAMES ROBERT ENTERLINE

1972
Garden City, New York
DOUBLEDAY & COMPANY, INC.

PLATE CREDITS

1 James Robert Enterline
2 Esther Enterline
3 V. N. Andreyev
4 J. Dewey Soper
5 Tyge W. Böcher
6 James Robert Enterline
7 James Robert Enterline
8 Danish National Museum, Ethnographical Department
9 Danish National Museum, Ethnographical Department
10 Danish National Museum, Ethnographical Department
11 Edward L. Moss
12 Royal Danish Ministry of Foreign Affairs
13 Edward L. Moss
14 National Museums of Canada
15 Joseph Fischer

Grateful acknowledgment is made to those who have given permission to reproduce the following material:

Physical Relief Map GH-2 reprinted with permission of the United States Air Force—Hq Aeronautical Chart and Information Center.

Excerpts from THE NORSE ATLANTIC SAGA by Gwyn Jones. Copyright © 1964 by Oxford University Press. Reprinted by permission of Oxford University Press.

Excerpts from LAND UNDER THE POLE STAR by Helge Ingstad. Copyright © 1966 by St. Martin's Press, Inc. Reprinted by permission of St. Martin's Press, Inc.

Excerpts from NEWFOUNDLAND LABRADOR by Vaino Tanner. Copyright 1947 by Cambridge University Press. Reprinted by permission of Cambridge University Press.

Excerpts from IN NORTHERN MISTS by Fridtjof Nansen. Copyright Heinemann 1911. *Reprinted by permission of Mrs. Odd Nansen.*

ISBN: 0-385-02585-8
Library of Congress Catalog Card Number 76-175370
Copyright © 1972 by James Robert Enterline

TO MY MOTHER

who taught me what dedication means

Foreword

By Gerard L. Alexander

When I was first invited to examine this revolutionary book on America's Viking heritage, I was curious. I recalled the moments of revelation I experienced reading the 1965 Yale University book, *The Vinland Map and the Tartar Relation,* and I wondered how another author could find anything new to say. The present author's contention, that previously unrecognized information exists in many old maps familiar to historical cartographers, turned my curiosity to fascination. He writes in a most readable and entertaining style, and constantly involves the reader in an unfolding detective story.

This is not just an entertaining book, however, but a fundamentally significant study of a key portion of man's history. Previous books on the Norse discovery of America have tended to concentrate on the sagas about Leif Eiriksson's discovery of "Vinland" around A.D. 1000, and they have generally ignored the five hundred years between that time and Columbus' discovery. The present book is primarily concerned with filling that gap. It examines the critical question of how much connection there was between the Norse and Columbian discoveries, and it presents a novel theory on the

location of Vinland. It succeeds in being the first overall
history of the Norse people in America.

In the process, the book introduces many ideas which are
bound to provoke discussion. It interprets unrecognizable
maps of alleged lands in Eurasia as being actual maps of
lands half a world away in America. It quotes barely com-
prehensible medieval descriptions of lands supposedly European, which descriptions become eminently clear when
applied to American settings. It marshalls a massive collection of evidence of misunderstood European notions about
American lands, extending down into the Columbian age of
discovery. If these ideas can withstand the scrutiny of scholars, they will have introduced a wholly unique aspect of
Western history.

In anticipation of such scrutiny, a planned separate volume of supportive evidence, which I have read in manuscript, presents the most thorough body of material on its
subject ever assembled. A unique chronological survey
therein examines nearly a hundred maps and documents in
detail, each of which is supplied with an individual bibliography. That planned volume also contains a separate bibliography of facsimile atlases and a general bibliography
which, together with the one herein, embodies by far the
most comprehensive and up-to-date collection of references
on the Viking presence in America ever assembled in English.

But never, in the present volume, does any scholarly ma-
chinery get in the way of the reader's enjoyment of Viking
adventure. The spirit of discovery is all-pervasive in the very
nature of the material as well as in the insights provided.

Much of the work in this study was done at the Research
Libraries of the New York Public Library and led to much
interesting discussion between the author and myself. All

who are interested in specialties such as history, archaeology, geography, anthropology or cartography—or just in the flow of human events, will welcome the author's efforts in print.

GERARD L. ALEXANDER

Chief, Map Division
The Research Libraries
New York Public Library

Contents

FOREWORD BY GERARD L. ALEXANDER   vii

AUTHOR'S PREFACE   xv

1. INTRODUCTION: THE LOST NATION OF GREENLAND   1

2. FINDING LEIF EIRIKSSON'S AMERICA   13

3. AT ISSUE: THE NORSE WORD "VINLAND"   29

4. THE NORSE STORY IN SAGA AND STONE   49

5. TRACES ON THE MAPS OF HISTORY   73

6. THE COLUMBUS CONTROVERSY   99

7. NORSEMEN AMONG THE ESKIMOS   115

8. THE NORSE DISPERSAL INTO CANADA   129

9. GREENLAND'S END AND AMERICA'S BEGINNINGS   147

EPILOGUE BY THOR HEYERDAHL   165

NOTES   183

BIBLIOGRAPHY   189

INDEX   203

Illustrations

PLATES

1 Eirik the Red's Farm in Greenland

2 Remains of Norse Greenlanders' Cathedral

3 Trees North of the Tree Line

4 The Landscape in Vinland

5 The Landscape in Markland

6 Greenland's Mile-Thick Icecap

7 Navigational Hazards from Sea Ice

8 Items Proving Norse/Eskimo Trade

9 Norse Remnants from Northernmost Greenland

10 Norse Ship Rigging Made by Eskimos

11 Norse Cairns from Island North of Canada

12 Inscribed Norse Stone from North Greenland

13 Norse Duck Shelter from Eastern Canadian Arctic

14 Norse Hut from Central Canadian Arctic

15 Norse Map of Western Alaska

MAPS

Endpapers: World Polar Geography

p. 50 The Setting of the Vinland Scenario

p. 89 Fifteenth Century Map/Modern Alaska Map Comparison

Author's Preface

Lately Stonehenge has been decoded, the Lost Atlantis has been found and King Arthur's Camelot has been located, so say some researchers. If so, that leaves the discovery of America as one of the few remaining mysterious romances of history. This book presents new evidence establishing the existence of continuing Norse explorations in America from Leif Eiriksson's time down to Columbus', and it shows that such explorations helped usher in Europe's Age of Discovery. Such an idea is completely at variance with all hitherto accepted theories, which looked upon Leif's contact with America as an isolated incident having no historical consequences. Thus, this book establishes for the first time the existence of a single continuum of European heritage in America for the past millennium. This fact will require a revision of the teaching of both American history and European history.

Sometime around A.D. 965 a red-headed adolescent immigrant to Iceland named Eirik probably began thinking about the prospects of having his own children. When his own children did arrive, they became destined, along with their father Eirik, to be the subject of several sagas telling of their geographical discoveries. A thousand years later in 1965 the newspapers carried an account of the acquisition by Yale University of an ancient world map, the so-called Yale Vinland Map, which depicted a land labeled "Vinland" to the west of Greenland. A caption on the map referred to these legendary Viking expeditions of Leif the Lucky and Eirik the Red, and the attempted settlement of the Norse colony of Vinland. In the face of much controversy, the parchment and penmanship of the map itself were authenticated by scholarly detective work as being of genuine pre-Columbian origin. However, the Yale editors' analysis of the unrecognizable coastline west of Greenland indicated that the map's "Vinland" seemed to be a mere conjectural rendition by medieval scholars of descriptions contained in the sagas.

My own study of six years has led me to believe that the Yale map does in fact depict real coastline data resulting from actual surveys; data which, however, was drawn on the map under the conditions of a systematic error. When I discovered the systematic distortion and analyzed it in detail and removed it, the coastline became quite recognizable as part of North America.

There are known to be many other geographical distortions present in the cartographic history of the Norsemen, particularly in the study of Scandinavia itself. In the course of my research, I examined these distortions in detail and in chronological sequence. As a result, many heretofore puzzling situations became clear. Above all, it became apparent that the Yale Vinland Map was only one of a long series of maps and other documents which told previously unknown stories of the history of the Norsemen and their explorations in North America. Many of these stories were verified during my field work in Greenland and Iceland.

This book is the general report of the many results of that study and of a new theory of Western history that they engendered. The theory proposes two theses that are contrary to established doctrine; first, that Leif Eiriksson's successors in Greenland eventually vacated that land and spread throughout North America, as far as Alaska, meanwhile sending to Europe geographical information that sparked Columbus' voyage. Second, that Leif Eiriksson's North American "Vinland" of A.D. 1000 was *not* a land of grapes on the temperate eastern seaboard but a land of pastures in nearly arctic Canada.

The book may be read for general interest in the subject, or serve as a reference or textbook for special courses. I have attempted to write in a non-technical style, but have not refrained from using standard technical terms where appropriate. Since the discussion at times necessarily becomes somewhat geographical, however, and involves regions perhaps somewhat unfamiliar to the reader, frequent reference to the map on the endpapers will be indispensable when such a discussion is encountered. I have endeavored to give as complete detailed arguments as possible for the primary conclusions reached, but I have not refrained from also making several intuitive speculations that may suggest further research or commentary. This approach at times necessarily suspends the modern scholarly critical standards, but hopefully I have nevertheless avoided much of the overzealous hysteria that this field of study has known.

While there are many specific elements in this book that elicit my thanks to others, no acknowledgment can overshadow that to my wife, Esther, without whose abiding faith and love and frequent active assistance this book would never have come to be. Gerard L. Alexander and his staff at the New York Public Library's Map Division have shown keen interest in the progress of my work almost since its inception, and his encouragement is directly responsible for its final completion. Others for whose interest I am thankful are Dr. Roman Drazniowsky and the staff at the American Geographical Society, where many useful facilities were provided me, and Dr. Walter Ristow and the staff of the Geography and Map Division of the United States Library of Congress, which was helpful to me on many occasions and contributed new material to my research. Dr. Thomas Marston and the staff of the Yale University Library provided encouragement and assistance in my study of the Yale Vinland Map, and Dr. Helen Wallis of the British Museum's Map Room was helpful on several occasions.

Warm thanks are also extended to all the people who contributed to success of my field work. In Greenland, Peter Fabricius of Greenlandair provided special transportation and guide service to the ruins of Gardar where useful photographic measurements were made, and Anna Panúm, hostess of the Arctic Hotel, was very helpful and informative about the modern communities that have sprung up among the ruins. Lars Motzfeldt, *lektor* of the contemporary settlement on Eirik the Red's farm site, guided me among the various excavations and very hospitably received me into his own home. In Iceland, Kristjan Jónsson and Magnus Hjartarson provided me with the opportunity for firsthand exposure to landmarks and conditions extending between Reykjavik and Skálholt. Information gained there has proven useful in understanding some of the Norse saga statements.

It is my lament that I was not equipped to read the vast literature in the original northern languages, but Dr. and

Mrs. John D'Emilio and Joyce Noriega provided assistance in translating various medieval southern dialects. (The final responsibility for errors, naturally, rests with myself.) The technical work of preparing the manuscript was assisted by many friends and acquaintances, including, at various times, a dozen different typists and research assistants. Thanks for reading and editing the manuscript at various stages are due to John Ware, Vivienne Millenson, Isabel Alter, Larry Fuld and, especially, Marsha Goldstein.

January 1972   *J. R. Enterline*
Salunga, Pennsylvania

VIKING
AMERICA

CHAPTER 1

Introduction: The Lost Nation of Greenland

America. Is it a country, a continent, a hemisphere? Or is it an age-old dream that has found reality? The ancient Celts in Ireland called themselves "Westmen" because they believed they inhabited the westernmost land in the world. Their own sailors eventually proved them wrong by sailing northwest across the open ocean and discovering the island shown on the endpaper map we now call Iceland. They evidently then decided that Iceland was surely the ultimate island of the earth, *"Ultima Thule."*

More than a millennium ago the Old Norse sailors from Norway discovered from these Celtic neighbors that Irish monks sought solitude in this ultimate island far to their north and west. Soon the Norsemen sought out this place for themselves.[1] Plumbing along with lead and line,[2] they felt their way along the slopes of a vast submarine mountain chain, and soon were led from the Faroe Islands to the Irish hideout in Iceland.[3] The Irish quickly fled elsewhere from the pagan Norsemen.* However, the latter were themselves

---

* Some writers believe the Irish themselves may have known about America. I acknowledge this as a possibility, as well as the possibility of even more widespread ancient knowledge of America as described,

soon enough Christianized,[5] and their direct descendants, still speaking the Norse language, are the modern inhabitants of Iceland. For five hundred years before Columbus' voyage the Norsemen also inhabited Greenland and, as is shown herein, made at least attempted migrations to the mainland of America. Their movements leave one facing the surprising question: Did Columbus really discover anything new and unknown?

The Norse migration was, actually, merely the end of an already established heritage. Aside from their viking raids for plunder, which they outgrew before the Greenland era, the Old Norsemen more so than any of their fellow Germanic peoples, felt the need for *lebensraum*. Ever since the latest glacial retreat their ancestors had been constantly on the move.[6] They had ancestors who inhabited the northern latitudes at least long enough to evolve a fair complexion, but the prehistoric ancestors of all the modern Germanic peoples are also presumed to have included a group of husbandry oriented "Cordware Culture" people who lived somewhere in the plains of southern Russia.[7] How long they were there or what their history was is uncertain because it must be divined from archaeological traces, but some two millennia before the classical Roman period, carrying with them an Indo-European language, they began to drift northwestward by various routes, ending in Scandinavia. There the descendent peoples finished out the New Stone Age, went through a glorious Bronze Age and by early Roman times entered well into the Iron Age. Then some unknown deterioration of native conditions[8] forced some of them to go on the move again. The result was the Great Teutonic Migration of the early centuries A.D.

---

for example, by Cyrus Gordon.[4] But the scope of my study here is restricted to the Norsemen.

This migration was not recorded by the Teutons themselves, for they had neither parchment nor paper, but rather
by people at outposts of the expanding Roman Empire
whom later waves encountered as they fled southward.
These various Germanic tribes circulated throughout Europe
looking for suitable new places to live, and each caused its
share of trouble in the process.[9] Eventually, however, they
began to settle down in various places to begin the long
difficult process of assimilation that was to continue through
the Dark Ages. Some settled near the Roman lands and became the ancestors of the modern south Germans and
Austrians. Others—perhaps less gregarious tribes—avoided
both the Latins and the High Germans and went back
northward to become the Dutch and Saxons. Some tribes
simply disappeared in or became absorbed by other cultures.
But the most intensely individualistic and isolationist people
from Scandinavia avoided contact with all these other
peoples, and from the earliest times had remained in Denmark, Sweden and Norway to claim lands they could call
their own. Some, in the northwest, even tended to minimize
contact with one another.

These northernmost Norsemen, living in the fiords (*viks*)
of the mountainous west coast of Scandinavia, found out by
the A.D. 800s that they were caught in a cul-de-sac. While
private property meant more to them than perhaps to any
of the other Scandinavian individuals, they occupied a
land that was only somewhat marginally habitable—a land
from which they could not retreat and beyond which they
would find only increasingly severe conditions. Further ag-
gravating the situation, their personalities were hypersensi-
tized to one another, and the slightest provocation was
cause for a bloody feud among them. The pagan system of
values[10] was still centered on individual assertion and sur-

vival of the fittest,[11] and the law was primarily concerned
with deciding winners of feuds and valuating lost lives.[12]
The law was individually administered by each local chieftain, and the mechanics for settling differences between
chieftains was almost non-existent. As an alternative to con-
stant feuding, the desire for privately owned living space
was strong indeed.

Thus, when the Norse sailors discovered the existence of
virtually uninhabited Iceland around A.D. 874, the move to
colonization of the island came immediately. It was spurred
by the general exodus of chieftains from the viks of Norway
when Harald Fairhair, against the Vikings' reactionary
wishes to retain their individual ultimate authority,[13] established himself as the first king over all Norway. Iceland
was then set up as a free state completely independent of
Norway,[14] and it soon developed the first democratic par-
liament in the world.

Of fundamental importance in this Norse colonization of
Iceland was the navigating ability their ancestors had
learned[15] in prehistoric times, island-hopping across the
Kattegat—on the endpaper map—from Denmark to Scandinavia, later directly crossing the Skagerrak to Norway, and
while traveling from one fiord to another in Norway. This
navigational ability was refined during the Viking era late
in the first millennium A.D. when long sea voyages were
made to pillage the Christian nations to the south. The improvement of techniques gained thereby was very much
analogous to the improvement in the Christian nations' navigational techniques when they later made similar voyages
to pillage the Meso-American Indian civilizations. But even
before this the Norsemen could tell where a river came
down from the land by the taste of the sea water, or they
could direct their square-sailed ships into winds that would

have stilled many a southern ship.[16] Most important of all,
they could go on with well-founded confidence when southern sailors would have wisely turned back from the unknown.

The highest peak on the east coast of Iceland has an elevation just under 7000 feet, and to someone at water level it
would be just visible over the horizon about a hundred
miles out at sea from it. Norse sailors were familiar with the
hard fact that landfall visibility cannot be significantly im-
proved by elevating the observer to the top of the mast and
so used more efficient ways of sighting distant land. They
carried with them cages of large black ravens whose sil-
houettes stood out clearly against the sky. After having
sailed a while, the sailors would release a raven. If the bird
climbed to his ceiling and then returned to the ship, they
knew that no land of any appreciable elevation was in sight
for almost two hundred miles. If after climbing a while the
bird then flew towards the rear, they knew that they were
still in sight of homeland. (And by watching his path they
also got an indication of their bearing angle from the home
shores.) If he instead flew forward, presumably toward unknown land, they followed him.[17]

One of the most surprising aspects of Old Norse navigation is the fact that the sailors did not originally make maps
or charts but rather memorized all their sailing directions in
terms of solar and stellar headings, latitudes and sailing
time. Perhaps one of the primary reasons for this is that they
did not have paper and did not know how to make parchment from animal skins. For this same reason, lack of writing materials, they also had no written literature. Neither
were they able to write down their laws, nor their history.
In spite of this lack of bulk writing material, they did develop a Runic alphabet, ultimately derived from an old

Etruscan alphabet,[18] which was specially adapted for chiseling short inscriptions on memorial stones, such as in Plate 12, or wood carvings, and for transmitting short messages on wax tablets.[19]

Thus, all of the body of learned information that was desirable to transmit from one generation to another had to be memorized and passed on orally. Not much is known about the safeguards the Norsemen took to ensure accuracy in this transmission,[20] but the indications are that their methods in this case were just as clever as their methods in navigation. The lack of parchment had no necessary connection with a lack of intelligence,[21] and these people had in the Norse civilization all the arts their contemporaries did[22] except written literature. (As an analogy, the Romans did not invent writing materials themselves but learned of them from the Semitic peoples.) Those Norsemen who proved to have the most reliable memories naturally got the job of preserving and passing on oral information, but they constantly had to prove their memories. In the area of law, for example, there was an annual gathering at which, by thirds, the entire body of the law was recited from a hilltop.[23] One can imagine the reaction of the competitors if the poor reciter got so much as one syllable wrong.[24] It is thought by scholars that Norse history was preserved in much the same way with frequent gatherings providing a testing ground for individuals' memory of history. Namely, except for that of kings, history tended to be circumscribed in family rather than national terms. The reciting of a family history was called a saga (saga: that which is said, i.e., "what they say about so-and-so"). The telling of the family saga, and the criticism of the telling thereof,[25] presumably provided not only entertainment for many a cold, dark winter day[26] but also an opportunity for each family member to memorize the family past, with, admittedly, various degrees of accuracy.

Today, with the absence of written history, we can only fantasize about the nature of saga-telling during the first millennium. Nevertheless, many scholars believe that the more interesting or more important families' stories became subjects for professional storytellers, who in later times would have been authors or writers, and that these men interacted in such a way as to preserve the sagas as accurately as the lawspeakers preserved law.[27]

Then in the twelfth century A.D. a southern invention of an origin predating even the twelfth century B.C., after having touched mainland Scandinavia the preceding century, finally reached the nation of Iceland. This was the general knowledge of how to make and use parchment.[28] It came simultaneously with the conversion of Iceland from the gods of Asgard[29] to Christianity by the English.[30] The impact on Iceland of this new contact with the "civilized" south was incredibly swift. A contemporary of the first bishop of Iceland, born in 1056, was called "Saemund the Learned," and rightly so, for he had received an education at the University of Paris. Unfortunately, the negative aspects of interaction with an advanced culture were also felt. The immediate successors of Saemund the Learned did adapt the Latin alphabet to the Old Norse language and, much to their credit, began the job of recording on parchment all the family sagas they could collect. But the unfortunate aspect of this new method of keeping history was that it relieved many of the long-standing cultural pressures for *oral* accuracy without introducing adequate new checks and balances on *literary* accuracy. Whatever might have been the accuracy of the oral versions of the sagas, the scribes quickly began "improving" and embellishing the stories. Soon there were several different versions of the same story.[31]

Much modern scholarly analysis has gone into the study of which portions, if any, of the surviving manuscripts are reliable reports of the original oral sagas, and particular attention has been given to one special group—those that relate the discovery of the lands on the endpaper map still farther to the west of Iceland shortly before A.D. 1000. The generally accepted version of the story of the first land discovered, as told by these sagas, is given in highly summarized form in the following paragraph:

A pre-Christian Icelandic farmer-chieftain by the name of Eirik Thorvaldsson *Rauda* (the Red) desired to retrieve some equipment he thought he had only loaned to a neighboring chieftain, but the neighbor refused to return it. A feud ensued in which people on each side were killed, and eventually popular opinion decided that Eirik had gone too far. At a special meeting, which was highly infiltrated by his opponents, a law was passed banishing Eirik from the community for three years. This happened about 982. Since he and his father had been previously outlawed from two other communities,* he evidently decided that his world was too crowded and he would seek new lands. He had heard the story of a sailor who had been blown by a storm far west of Iceland, had found some skerries (now evidently volcanically destroyed) and had sighted land on the western horizon. Eirik, with his family, intended to look

---

* Not necessarily because they were unusually obnoxious, but rather because obnoxiousness was usual. Iceland's original settlers were also outlaws. To be an outlaw meant, literally, to be outside the *protection* of the law and thus fair game for anybody. Accordingly, outlaws were always allowed a certain grace period to flee for their safety with their families and slaves.

for that land. He also intended, if he found it, to return to Iceland at the end of his three-year sentence and pick up several of his friends to form a new colony. Events proceeded exactly as Eirik had planned, and in order to entice farmers to his new-found colony, he named it Greenland. During the first summer of colonization twenty-five ships set sail from Iceland to the southern tip of Greenland, following a route on the endpaper map northwest across Denmark Strait and then south along the Greenland coast and around the cape, to the always ice-free coast on the west side. Soon another thriving independent Norse republic was in existence there.

This settlement in Greenland, along with Iceland, became Christianized[32] and flourished until the middle 1400s. After that, while Iceland continued, the Greenland settlement strangely disappeared under circumstances on which this writer hopes to shed more light.*

The idea that a place with the icy reputation of Greenland could be an attractive place to live may seem incredible. The explanation for it is that the reputation is partly undeserved. The famous icecap of Greenland depicted in Plate 6, in fact, is not caused by its northerly latitude. Indeed, the southern tip of Greenland is at almost the same latitude as the northern tip of Scotland, and most of the parts settled by Norsemen were no more northerly than

* However, the complete history of this medieval "free state" of Greenland is not my main purpose here since it has been more than adequately explored by many other writers. One of the most informative of these is Daniel Brunn in his monograph "The Icelandic Colonization of Greenland," published in English in Volume 57 of *Meddelelser om Grönland*. One of the most smoothly reading popular accounts is Vilhjalmur Stefansson's *Greenland*, and perhaps the most intimate account is Helge Ingstad's *Land Under the Pole Star*.

modern-day Oslo or Helsinki. And all of them were more
southerly than relatively "balmy" Iceland with its oceanic
climate. The icecap is caused, rather, by the extreme elevations of the Greenland interior, which are indicated on the
endpaper map.

While it is true that *almost* all of Greenland is covered
with eternal ice, it is also true that Greenland is the largest
island in the world. This large island happens to include an
ice-free lowlands area equivalent to the size of Great Brit-
ain.[33] While this land does not support any significant
growth of trees, there is, as shown in Plate 2, much grass,
and it is indeed green in summertime. Most early modern
explorers were able to penetrate the vast tracts of the north
only because they went in wintertime when travel by dog
sled was relatively easy, and thus the most memorable picture we have received from them of Greenland is a winter
picture. Since the advent of the airplane we have come to
understand that summer does reach even the Arctic. The
lowlands, even at the very *northern* tip of Greenland, support, in summertime, wild oxen grazing among meadow
flowers pollinated by bees.

Indeed, the Norse settlers in the lowlands of the southerly
west coast found conditions quite satisfactory for dairy farming. When I was there in the month of June I found day-
times pleasantly reminiscent of more southerly springtimes
and evenings reminiscent of fall. Winters of course are cold,
but not as cold as might be expected. They have been
described as similar in chill to Maine winters and certainly
milder than Minnesota winters.[34] Modern sheep farmers in
Greenland frequently leave their stock out over winter if
the snow does not cover the dead grass too deeply for them
to uncover.

The ruins of what were actually the two main Norse settlements in Greenland have been discovered, one at modern Julianehaab on the endpaper map and the other at Godt-haab. The east coast of the island was evidently avoided then as now because the persistent current from the polar basin creates pack-ice problems, depicted in Plate 7, regard-less of the season of the year. But the ruins on the west coast have been excavated[35] and appear to have provided a base for a completely comfortable home life.

The independent republic in Greenland in its turn also became a base for still further steps of exploration and movement. It is this further exploration that has stimulated romantic imaginations down through the ages, for these Greenland-based explorations seem to have reached Amer-ica. Such further movement is described in the sagas. My summary of that description follows:

Around 985, a few summers after Eirik's founding of Greenland, one Bjarni Herjolfsson, the adult son of one of Iceland's newly departed Greenland colonists, received the news belatedly and attempted to find his way from Iceland to his father's intended farm at the southern tip of Green-land. Bjarni was caught in bad weather and strayed south, then west, of his hearsay course directions to Greenland. He eventually sighted land, but recognizing that it could not be Greenland he turned around and pressed toward where he thought his father's farm should be. Before finally stumbling onto Greenland itself he made two more landfalls, which he did not investigate. This anecdote circulated widely in the Greenland settlement, and after some years Eirik's son Leif decided to investigate this land which lay even beyond Greenland. Around 1000 he bought or leased Bjarni's ship with its already experienced crew and sailed Bjarni's original discovery course in reverse, from Greenland

to the three sighted lands. He named the three lands Helluland (Slatestoneland), Markland (Timberland), and the
southernmost, Vinland.

According to some subsequent scholars but not by Leif's
explicit claim, the name "Vinland" was given to the land
because it grew vines bearing grapes for wine. This is
only one theory, and the reader should keep his mind open
for the alternate possible meaning of "pastureland" investigated in Chapter 3 of this book.

Subsequent voyages to Vinland as recorded in the sagas
were made by Leif's brother Thorvald; by a well-to-do
Icelandic trader, Thorfinn *Karlsefni* (The Valiant), who
married the widow of Leif's eldest brother Thorstein; and by
Leif's illegitimate half-sister, Freydis. Complete English
texts of these so-called Vinland sagas may be found in Gwyn
Jones's cited work, Magnusson and Palsson's, and many other
books. They are known as the *Saga of Eirik the Red,* otherwise called *Karlsefni's Saga,* and the *Tale of the Greenlanders.* * My own detailed analysis of the Vinland sagas is
given in Chapter 4.

The history of Viking America subsequent to the Vinland
voyages is treated in the second half of this book. Chapters
5 and 6 investigate the influence of the Norse explorations
on European history, and the last three chapters are devoted to tracing the wanderings in America of the ex-
patriates of the lost nation of Greenland.

* The foundation for modern critical scholarly analysis of these Vinland sagas was laid in Arthur Reeves' book *The Finding of Wineland
the Good,* and Fossum[36] and Merrill[37] have given surveys of several
important early analysts of the subject. The highly controversial
subject of saga research in general has recently been surveyed by
Andersson.[38]

CHAPTER 2

Finding Leif Eiriksson's America

At what spot did the Norsemen first set foot in America? In other words, where was the place the sagas called "Vinland?"

Helge Ingstad[1] has excavated some exciting Norse ruins at L'Anse au Meadows on the northern tip of Newfoundland which many writers have taken to be the remains of Vinland. I do not believe that L'Anse au Meadows was Vinland. I see no evidence besides wishful thinking supporting such an identification. In fact, the interpretations of the saga necessary to justify L'Anse au Meadows as Vinland seem rather strained; it is particularly difficult to imagine Leif sailing his ship up into Black Duck Brook, whatever the tide condition. The site proves, nevertheless, that Norsemen did reach America at the time of the sagas.[2]

In accounting for this site, one should not overlook another Christian land of other sagas which was supposed to be south of Vinland, *Hvitramannaland*.[3] This "Land of White Men" was referred to in other sagas as "Great Ireland" and may reflect a tradition of Irish contact with America before Vinland. It was evidently a mixture very

familiar in those days of Irish and Norse, but at least one
part of it was presumably strictly Norse: that which, according to the saga, was occupied by an Icelander named
Ari Marsson. The story is that he, along with the standard
ship's complement of those days which comprised entire
families, was driven by storms around A.D. 980 to a now unknown place which the saga referred to familiarly as *Hvitramannaland*. This was described in a later saga as being
"behind Vinland" (i.e., south of it) and located six days'
sailing west of Ireland. There Ari and his fellow castaways
settled permanently. L'Anse au Meadows, at the northern
tip of Newfoundland, lies exactly due west after rounding
the southern coast of Ireland, actually seven days of ordinary Norse sailing away. One piece of charcoal retrieved
from the ruin at L'Anse au Meadows was carbon dated at
A.D. 900[4] and another at 890,[5] more than a century before
the Vinland era. Nevertheless, according to the saga *Hvitramannaland* was supposed to have been inhabited even
before Ari Marsson's time. There is a distinct possibility that
L'Anse au Meadows was *Hvitramannaland*. I concur, in any
case, with Carl Sauer's and others' reluctance to conclude
that it was Vinland.[6] Indeed, in spite of a natural desire that
it be so, Ingstad himself has refrained from such a conclusion in print.[7]

Ever since Thorfinn Karlsefni set out on the track of Leif
Eiriksson in the early 1000s, people have been searching
unsuccessfully for the location of Vinland. As is evidenced
by a variety of Vinland maps in several museums, even
early scholars close to the Norsemen seem to have disagreed
about its location.

The sagas contain statements about Vinland's location,
but they are couched in the framework of descriptions of
other lands explored on the same trip, Markland and Hel-

luland. Thus, in order to locate Vinland with confidence one must first locate Markland and Helluland. The easiest of these to locate is the one that was supposed to be the closest to Greenland, Helluland.

Scholars agree universally in interpreting Helluland as Baffin Island, just west of Greenland on the endpaper map. The reason is partly because of this island's physical characteristics. The east coast of Baffin Island is second only to Greenland in the extent of its glaciers, and it lacks Greenland's saving grace of habitable lowlands near the coast. The *Tale of the Greenlanders* describes Leif's encounter with Helluland thus:

They sailed to land there, cast anchor and put off a boat, then went ashore, and could see no grass there. The background was all great glaciers, and right up to the glaciers from the sea as it were a single slab of rock. The land impressed them as barren and useless. "At least," said Leif, "it has not happened to us as to Bjarni over this land, that we failed to get ourselves ashore. I shall now give the land a name, and call it Helluland [land of crags]." After which they returned to the ship.[8]

Bjarni Herjolfsson's original encounter with Helluland is described in this way:

. . . and then they saw the third land, and this land was high, mountainous and glaciered. They asked whether Bjarni would put ashore there, but no, he said, he had no wish to. "For to me this land looks good for nothing." So without so much as lowering their sail they held on along the land, and came to see that it was an island.[9]

These physical descriptions of the great glaciers and vast cliffs are uniquely applicable to Baffin Island (outside of Greenland), and when combined with sailing directions in the sagas they make the prevailing theory that Helluland was on Baffin Island seem completely acceptable. But there is certainly no reason to believe, just because of the last phrase quoted above, that Bjarni *circumnavigated* Baffin Island or even sailed along its thousand-mile length. Bjarni was in a hurry to get to Greenland, and his refusal to stop anywhere for water or supplies after already having been detained would have completely ruled out any such possibility. The "island" to which Bjarni was referring could not have been the whole of Baffin Island, but his "Helluland" might still have been a specific part of Baffin Island.

The possibility of an offshore island with a glacier must be ruled out, for all of Baffin's offshore islands (except in the far north, which the sagas' sailing directions rule out) are too low to maintain permanent ice. Thus, it begins to seem rather likely that Helluland was actually on one of the glaciated mountainous peninsulas of Baffin's mainland, appearing on the endpapers, which Bjarni mistook to be completely insulated. Perhaps he did not really "come to see that it was an island," but rather came to *believe* that it was an island when he saw water on three sides of it and was unable to see Baffin's mainland over the horizon. Indeed, the unusually long promontories of Baffin Island and the unusually extended bays between them have confused many explorers. When Frobisher discovered Frobisher Bay, the southernmost of the endpaper map, he surmised it to be an entrance to the Northwest Passage. And members of his expedition later convinced themselves that Hudson Strait and Frobisher Bay met one another at their northwestern ends, so that the southernmost Meta Incognita Peninsula (recently renamed the Frobisher Peninsula) seemed to them an island.[10] Subsequent explorers maintained such inaccuracies down to the middle of the nineteenth century when explorers like Ross began to dispel them.

All three of Baffin Island's southeast-pointing peninsulas have some glaciated areas, but by far the most likely to be widely visible from out at sea is that of the Cumberland Peninsula, the northernmost of the three. Here some glaciated areas come down to within a few miles of the open Davis Strait, and in the background the icecap rises to 7000 feet or more. The stark rock cliffs rise straight out of the water, with none of the signs of soil bearing tundra growth such as are present on the other two prominences.[11] One must surely agree with Bjarni, if this is really where he was, that "this land looks good for nothing."

It may be noted on the endpaper map that this particular prominence, Cumberland Peninsula, is north of the Western Settlement (modern Godthaab) while the other two are south of it, nearer the Eastern Settlement (Julianehaab). I think it is significant that when Karlsefni wanted to go from the Eastern Settlement to Helluland he first sailed northward, past the Western Settlement:

They then sailed away for the Western Settlement and for Bjarneyjar [somewhere north of the Western Settlement, perhaps Disko Island near Svartenhuk]. From Bjarneyjar they sailed with a north wind, were at sea two days, and then found land. They rowed ashore in boats and explored the country, finding great stone slabs there, many twelve ells wide. There were many white foxes there. They gave the land a name, calling it Helluland.[12]

The prevailing winds in Davis Strait are from the north, and the fact that they sailed with a north wind would only seem to indicate that they had planned their journey sufficiently well to enable them to start out for Helluland on a typical

day. But the currents in this part of Davis Strait are also
from the north. Thus, if the initial leg northward beyond the
Western Settlement was an inherent part of the journey to
Helluland, as the saga seems to indicate it was, then it must
have been for the purpose of compensating for these south-
tending components. This implies that Helluland was not
just any part of Baffin Island, but most likely, in fact,
Cumberland Peninsula. The two days at sea with a beam
wind and current might be about right for such a journey
across the narrow part of Davis Strait.

A final confirmation of the identification of Helluland
as Cumberland Peninsula can be obtained by following
Bjarni's entire course on the endpaper map from its origin
in Iceland. His intended course would first have taken him
northwestward across Denmark Strait until Greenland was
well in sight. Only then should he have turned southward
and followed the coast over five hundred miles to his father's
farm at the southern tip. But, says the saga, before he had a
chance to sight Greenland at all, bad weather cut off his
visibility and began drifting him southward. He must have
tried to ride out the bad weather, but before relenting it
took him below the end of Greenland and then westward.
However, he was not aware of the westerly drift, only the
southerly. When Bjarni now attempted to regain his proper
northerly starting latitude, he was sailing northward in the
waters to the *west* side of Greenland. When he reached the
latitude of Cumberland Peninsula, he would have been at
the same latitude as his proper starting place, Denmark
Strait on the opposite side of Greenland. Then he would
have been forced to realize, since the coastline here on Baffin Island did not answer the description of Greenland, that
he must have somehow circumnavigated Greenland. The

saga tells us that he now turned around and, sailing before
a fresh wind, went directly to the southern tip of Greenland
in four days.[13] This seems just the right length of time for
such a voyage from the Cumberland Peninsula.

I conclude that Helluland was specifically the Cumberland Peninsula of Baffin Island.

The next land south after Helluland was Markland, the
"wooded land." Those who wish to believe that the actual
location of Vinland was somewhere in the presently highly
developed areas of modern white man will now be holding
tightly to the sagas' statements that Vinland was supposed
to be south of Markland. Markland has been identified by
all writers on the subject, unquestioningly up to this point,
with the towering forests of Labrador, so that Vinland, these
writers say, must at least be south of Labrador. But they
must now release their clutch on this cherished, romantic
idea. Markland, and therewith Vinland, must be relocated
northward. For, a few questions must be asked regarding
what the phrase "wood land" meant to a Greenlander, and
the answers will show that identifying Markland as Labrador is jumping to a conclusion.

The *Hauksbok* version of Eirik the Red's saga says with
regard to the sample trees brought back from the new lands:

Some of the trees were so big that they were used in housebuilding.[14]

Some of the trees, mind you, were so big. *So* big. This does
not say very much that is favorable about most of the trees
in Markland. Evidently the unexceptional trees were *not*
big enough to be used in housebuilding. Such a scarcity of
large trees is hardly characterisitic of the towering Labrador

forest. But the argument for the location of Markland in
Labrador becomes even weaker when it is realized just how
small a tree could be to be of usefulness in the building of a
Greenlander's house. The Greenlanders did not build board
or log houses, but did all their construction in stone and
turf.[15] The only real use made of trees in housebuilding was
as posts[16] to hold up a low roof, frequently of woven light
twigs and turf, or perhaps leather, covering. Thus, "so big
that they were used in housebuilding" probably refers to
trees about fifteen feet tall at the most.

A "wood land" in which the *exceptional* trees are about
fifteen feet tall is just what one finds at various places
throughout the Arctic above the tree line. The idea that
trees cannot grow north of the tree line is a popular misconception about the real meaning of the tree line. The reasons for the sharpness of the tree line have to do with the
way each kind of vegetation, tree or tundra, simultaneously
provides for the protection of its own seedlings and dis-
courages the seedlings of all others.[17] The Arctic, of course,
has a built-in bias against trees with its sudden winds and
short growing season, but aside from this, once a soil area is
claimed by tundra there is a self-maintaining process of (1)
choking of any tree seedlings by tundra grass, and (2)
eventually, the lack of a source of further tree seeds. If conditions such as terrain shelter from winds are satisfactory,
however, and trees from bird-transported seeds can gain a
foothold, then they can shade out the tundra and take over
the soil area themselves. Such "forest islands" in the tundra
are an analogue of clearings in forests at familiar altitudes
and latitudes, and are scattered widely beyond the tree line,
as shown in Plates 3 and 4.

While the area covered by these "forest islands" can become considerable as one goes southward toward the tree line, the individual trees seldom attain anything more than scrub height. The explorer Dewey Soper found the stands of twelve-foot Planifolia willows of Plate 4 in south-central Baffin Island,[18] and other writers have speculated that birch, spruce and larch of similar height may be found on sheltered south-facing slopes of Baffin which have July and August temperatures of 50° or more.[19] The "great forest of Greenland," which is mentioned in several sagas with pride, is an isolated growth of birches not over twenty feet tall.[20]

Such growths are, nevertheless, not commonplace, and are unquestionably remarkable to see when encountered. Except for the just mentioned birch grove in one isolated fiord, the Greenlanders were used to the landscape of Plates 1 and 2 which contained nothing but low grasses and willow shrubs in soil areas and nothing but bare rock on mountaintops. After the similar barrenness which the saga says the explorers encountered in Helluland before reaching Markland, even the stunted growth of an arctic "forest island" would have been an exciting sight, and the naming of such a place as "Markland" would have been quite in order. The famous explorer and film maker Robert Flaherty described such clumps of dwarf trees as "inexpressibly welcome."[21] Nowhere in the sagas is the "forest" of Markland compared at all favorably with the "forest" of Greenland, and Hauk Erlendsson's comment about housebuilding suggests just the opposite. Many modern translators insist on placing the adjective "great" in front of the forest of Markland,[22] but the original manuscripts contain no such adjective, merely saying that the land was found to sustain a growth of wood (*fundu land skògvaxit*).[23]

Further evidence to support this conclusion is contained

in the Greenlanders' tale's description of Karlsefni's antici-
pated encounter with hostile natives in Vinland, who had
the nasty habit of sneaking about a nearby "woods" without
warning. Karlsefni knew from a previous incident that the
natives were afraid of his cattle, and reasoned thus:

So let us follow this plan, that ten men move forward on to the
ness here, letting themselves be seen, while the rest of our
company go into the wood to clear a passage there for our
cattle, in readiness for when their host advances from the wood.
Also we must take our bull and let him march at our head.[24]

This may sound like a good plan, but the ten men on the
headland would have been endangered for a good many
hours if Karlsefni really had been talking about chopping
down trees in a forest of the Labrador type with Norse bat-
tle axes, actually the size of hatchets.[25] Furthermore, in
such a forest there would have been no need to clear a
passage for the cattle, as the trunks of trees in such a forest
are generally well separated. However, in any extensive
arctic "forest island" of thickly grown scrub such a passage
would be quite necessary, and at the same time it would
have been within the capability of the Norse axes to hack a
passage through the thin trunks and branches as they
marched.

The sagas make specific mention of certain wood-covered
headlands and wooded coasts in a context where such mention seems, in the older theory on Markland, quite irrele-
vant; namely, in a sequence of segments of sailing directions.
It now becomes clear that these woodlands were not mentioned for the purpose of praising the scenery in Markland,
but actually were part of the directions. They served as a
landmark for the sailors because the occasional wooded

areas found were quite the exception rather than the rule
in Markland. The sagas' sailing directions say:

. . . afterward sailed away and east along the land, and into the
mouth of the next fiord they came to, and to a headland jutting
out there which was all grown with woods.[26]

Note that the only information needed to specify *which*
headland was meant was the mention of its wood cover. At
another place:

. . . They went north past Kjalarnes, and then bore away west,
with the land on their port side. There was one single wilderness
to be seen ahead with hardly a clearing anywhere. [These
excited words seem to describe an exceptional condition.] And
when they had been on their travels at length, there was a river
flowing down off the land from east to west [notice, now not
flowing invisibly through the previous wilderness].[27]

While it seems clear that these "forests" were isolated
arctic "forest islands" which served as landmarks, it nevertheless also seems from the description that they were more
frequently encountered and more extensive than what one
would find today in Baffin Island, for example, where trees
such as in Plate 4 are quite a rarity. Today one must look to
the Cape Chidley or Ungava area of northern Quebec, on
the endpaper map, for appropriate tree conditions.[28] However, only a very slight difference in climate is enough to
have a profound effect on these growths hovering at the
margin of existence. A degree less might eliminate them
completely, and a degree more might allow them to prolif-
erate. If one accepts the theories of a "secondary climatic
optimum" around A.D. 1000,[29] then these scenes could well
have taken place somewhere on Baffin Island.

To help settle this question of Baffin Island versus Quebec
as the locale for these scenes, it is useful to recall the conclusion that Helluland was on Baffin Island. When the conclusion that Helluland was *specifically* on the Cumberland
Peninsula is recalled, then one is immediately confronted
with an interesting numerical situation on the endpaper
map. Namely, southward from Helluland there are two more
peninsulas of Baffin Island to account for and two more
saga lands to account for—Markland and Vinland. Is it possible that Markland was the middle peninsula of Baffin
Island? The modern explorer Weeks may have echoed Leif's
and Bjarni's differentiation between Helluland and Markland when he said:

As one travels westward across Cumberland Sound a very
marked change is apparent in the character of the country:
the mountains markedly decrease in height; steep rugged cliffs
are not so numerous.[30]

It must be realized that the name "Markland" did not necessarily mean that that land consisted only of trees, but perhaps trees were its primary asset *in comparison with Helluland*.[31] Markland was the first land to be named by Leif
following the wastes of Helluland, and the proper choice of
a name would have been one which most emphasized its
contrast with Helluland. To a Greenlander, this contrast
would have been most clearly seen in the trees, small
though they may have been. (Once the name "Markland"
was given, it would have stuck even though much larger
trees may have been found later in Vinland. In fact, the
"trees" which Leif brought back and which were used in
housebuilding were most certainly the more choice ones
from the more southerly Vinland.) An even greater impor-

tance of wood to the Greenlanders than for housebuilding
was for its use as fuel. It is recorded that they quickly de-
nuded the areas surrounding their settlements of all scrub
with woody branches, regardless of size. One such woody
growth, the Arctic willow, with branches a yard long and
an inch or more in diameter, is one of the most common
plants in the Arctic, and frequently precedes other plants,
even grasses, in spreading to and producing new soils in
rock crevices.[32] Various low willow species abound in the
Arctic,[33] and when they become cross-pollinated the phenomenon of hybrid vigor makes them appear more as trees
than bushes. Such hybrid willows as in Plate 5 are quite
eye-catching as one sails along an otherwise empty coastline. Such trees can be found even nowadays on the middle
Hall Peninsula of Baffin and throughout the island. The
Planifolia willow, the one that would have been useful in
housebuilding, does not occur this far north, but does occur
on the southernmost peninsula of Baffin Island.[34] Growths
of scrub no taller than a man and useful for little except fuel
or cover are the natural "forests" of modern Iceland, and
they are named with the same Norse word used by the
sagas in describing Markland, *skógr*. While the original
forests of Iceland may have been more substantial,[35] the
Greenlanders were in no position to be contemptuous of any
wood growths at all.

Another Old Norse word used in the sagas in connection
with the wood has also misled many writers. The trees were
said to be of *mösurr* wood, which in modern Icelandic
means "maple." Edward Gray points out, however, that this
meaning is of strictly modern evolution, and that originally the word meant, simply, "gnarled."[36] This adjective
applies very well to the arctic and sub-arctic scrub growths,
which become very twisted and intertwined. In another un-

related saga, *mösurr* trees are described as being found far
north in Finmark, so far beyond the tree line that any existing trees must have been scrubs.[37] That this descriptive
meaning, "gnarled," rather than a species identification was
intended in the sagas, is suggested by Karlsefni when, at the
end of the *Tale of the Greenlanders,* he sells some kind of
wooden instrument as a souvenir to a visitor. It is there
stated that Karlsefni did not know what kind of wood it was,
but that nevertheless it was *mösurr* wood from Vinland.[38]
This instrument had an obscure Norse name *husasnotrotre*
which translates literally as "house-neat-wood" and which
some writers have suggested interpreting as "broom."[39]
This interpretation would jibe very well with the interpretation of *mösurr* as stunted arctic trees, for a bundle of willow
branches would form a most functional broom.

In any case, the real Markland must not have had the
kind of interest for the explorers that the Labrador forest
would have. For, after giving Markland its name, they "got
back down to the ship as fast as they could."[40] This mod-
eration of interest suggests that modern writers may be
jumping again to conclusions when they become excited
about certain other features of Markland now to be examined. Before leaving, the explorers did make a cursory
examination on foot:

The country was smooth and grown with wood, with white
sands widely wherever they went, and shelving gently to the
sea.[41]

The mention of white sands has been seized upon by many
writers who wished to see Markland in Labrador, and who
identified the sands with a certain forty-mile beach in Labrador.[42] They were also identified with what may be an en-

tirely different beach in Karlsefni's voyage, *Furdustrandir*.[43]
These identifications are not justified. Just because the saga
used the word *vìda* (widely) as an adverb (*not* an adjective) does not necessarily mean that the sands themselves had to extend forty miles or be of hourglass quality
sand. One must see the concept "widely scattered" through
the eyes of an explorer on foot in a completely new land. In
fact, after the plunging cliffs of Helluland any beach at all
would have been considered extensive. Perhaps it will be
just as surprising to the modern reader as it may have been
to Leif, to find that there is actually a part of the eastern
end of the middle peninsula of Baffin Island that shelves
more or less gently to the sea. This is the eight or ten miles
of coast just south and west of Cape Haven, Hall Peninsula's
east-central tip, at 62°55′ N. Here the land shelves gently
back from the sea with an overall slope of less than 1 in 10
for miles inland, and although I have not been able to make
an on-site inspection, aerial photographs show the widespread existence of beaches and sand bars.

The trouble with any attempt to identify Markland as the
Cape Haven area is that there are many other areas of Baffin, including the southernmost Frobisher Peninsula, that
contain places answerable to the physical description of
Markland. What one needs in order to isolate one particular
candidate for identification, as Markland, from the others is
a set of sailing directions with detail that would apply to
that candidate alone. Unfortunately, in the case of Markland the sagas contain almost no detailed sailing directions,
and one is left with only the previous numerical observation
that there are three peninsulas of Baffin Island and three
saga lands.

Thus, it seems proper to turn at this point to the question
of whether it is possible that Vinland was the lower penin-

sula of Baffin Island. But this question appears absurd to
proponents of the interpretation of Vinland as "Wineland,"
because grapes cannot grow nearly this far north. Before
addressing this question, it is necessary to convince such
proponents that an alternate interpretation of Vinland is
valid.

CHAPTER 3

At Issue: The Norse Word "Vinland"

In pre-Columbian times, a romantic aura attached to the word "Vinland" boosted the land's importance out of all proportion to the attention it would have otherwise received. The romantic aura seems to have its earliest recorded expression in Adam of Bremen who in 1076 said:

. . . is called Wineland because vines grow there of themselves and give the noblest wine. And that there is abundance of unsown corn (grain) we have obtained certain knowledge, not by fabulous supposition, but from trustworthy information of the Danes.

Such a story had immediate acceptance throughout Europe, for as the age of the epic romances was coming into being, seekers of various earthly paradises eagerly consumed, and in fact embellished, all available legends. That age has now long since passed, but in some quarters there remain two vestiges of it: interests in chivalry and Vinland "the Good." Indeed, the very origin of the so-called "American dream" lies in a romantic continuation of a desire for the earthly paradise.[1] Adam of Bremen's assertion that Vinland was so-named because it had grapevines has been one of the primary sources cited in most modern attempts to locate it and has resulted in theories, like those of Frederick J. Pohl, placing it as far south as Cape Cod, Massachusetts, or even Virginia. In modern times, such theories have a romance of their own, based on the desire of the current inhabitants of the various candidate localities to share vicariously in the discovery of America.

I must beg such inhabitants' pardon for intending to deny them that experience. I intend to show that "Vinland" did not mean "wineland," but rather "pastureland." And I intend to show that it was located in the very northernmost part of Canada.

Adam's interpretation of the meaning of "Vinland" has been questioned by other writers[2] because of its similarity to his highly simplistic explanation of Greenland: "The people are blueish green from the salt water; and from this the region takes its name." It is known from Eirik the Red's own statement that, in fact, he chose the name Greenland to attract colonists. Aside from this comment on Adam's use of inventiveness in the description of Greenland, other "internal evidence" from his two statements quoted previously deserves critical scrutiny. The first statement, which contains rather astounding information about noble wine, is made simply as an a priori assertion of truth with no proof offered to back it up. However, the second statement containing the much less surprising information about wild grain has been defended by the phrase, "we have obtained certain knowledge, not by fabulous supposition, but from trustworthy information of the Danes." Why would Adam have found such a defensive attitude necessary if he did not anticipate that his reader would suspect him of having already engaged in fabulous supposition concerning the meaning of "Vinland"?

The old Norse word "Vinland" was indeed a challenge to interpret since the language spoken by the mainland Scandinavians in Adam's time actually contained no such word. To this eleventh-century scholar of Latin, the temptation must have been strong to make it "Vine-land" or "Wine-land" and spell it in Norse as a Latin word with a long *i*— *Vínland*. However, the reality is that the medieval Norsemen had little knowledge of either grapes or wine. In spite of isolated cases of importing by sophisticated traders, the Greenlanders knew neither how to make wine nor how to drink it. Their only alcoholic beverage was a kind of heavy mead or beer. In fact, except within the manuscripts of the sagas, which were written long after Adam's eleventh-century pronouncement, the only other occurrence in all of early Norse literature of such a Latin-based word with a long *i*, meaning wine, is in the Stjórn translation of the Bible.[3] The only later reference to wine in Greenland is to the unsuccessful attempt of a bishop returning from the European mainland to carry out King Sverre's recipe for crowberry wine.[4]

Nevertheless, there can be no doubt that the name originally referred to some kind of vegetation. For one thing, Karlsefni evidently made his search for Leif's Vinland by tracing the native vegetation. For another thing, the context of the sagas makes it clear that vegetation was being referred to. Using boldfaced type in the following quotations for words temporarily translated in the classical wine-oriented way from originals that contain the root *vin*, the oldest known variant of the *Saga of Eirik the Red* says:

There [at a place called Hop] they found self-sown fields of wheat where the ground was low-lying, and **vines** wherever it was hilly.[5]

The *Hauksbok* version of the return of Karlsefni's two runners who discovered similar vegetation is:

. . . the one had a bunch of grapes in his hand and the other
an ear of new-sown wheat.[6]

Leif's original discovery is described thus:

There were wheat-fields growing wild there and vines too.[7]

While it is clear from this literary context that the root
word *vin* referred to some kind of vegetation, it would seem
from the previously cited historical context that it may be
jumping to a conclusion to translate it as vines, grapes or
wine-berries. Various writers including Nansen, Hovgaard
and Ingstad have been disturbed by this jumping to conclusions and have examined this possibility: that the original, now lost manuscripts contained a truly Norse word
which was *not* spelled with a long *i*, and that the name
"Vinland" with a *short i* actually was based on the archaic
Old Norse word for *pasture*.[8] However, many quickly rejected the possibility that *vin* equaled pasture on the
grounds that philologists supposed that that word, with a
short *i*, had completely disappeared from the Norse language before the eleventh century. I would like to present
several reasons why the meaning *vin*=pasture should not
be rejected, but rather accepted as the valid linguistic interpretation.

First, while the word with a short *i* may have passed out
of use by literati on the mainland before the eleventh century, we have no idea of what words were being spoken by
simple farmers isolated in Iceland, Greenland or beyond.
In fact, such a situation is ideal for the preservation of

archaic linguistic patterns, as witness modern Icelandic in its near preservation of Old Norse. Certainly, one must admit of at least a possibility of the meaning *vin*=pasture being retained somewhere in the spoken language, since the written language with which philologists are forced to deal was produced by an entirely different class of people than the Viking settlers of the western lands. And these political reactionaries conceivably were just as reactionary in their spoken language as in their politics. Analysis of place names shows that the old word *vin* was clung to in at least some outlying localities.[9]

Second, the meaning of *vin* as pasture makes far more practical sense in historical context than does any other meaning proposed, for when the Norse ships arrived at a new landfall, pastureland would have been one of their most important finds. Why? Because the open, undecked Viking ships usually carried cattle aboard. Adam of Bremen himself described the Norse dependence on cattle thus:

Nortmannia is on account of its stony mountains or its immoderate cold the most infertile of all regions, and only suited to rearing cattle. The cattle are kept a long time in the waste lands, after the manner of the Arabs. They live on their herds, using their milk for food and their wool for clothes.[10]

With no grain available to make bread, the only source of sea-going carbohydrates was cheese and the milk of hay-fed cattle. *Hauksbok* explicitly mentions that cattle were taken along on shipboard on the early exploratory voyages to Iceland,[11] and Nansen theorizes that it was the search for pastureland that forced Eirik the Red to abandon his first landfall on Greenland and search for a more adequate herding place.[12] It is also known by explicit statement that

Karlsefni had all kinds of livestock along on his voyage to Vinland.[13] Under such conditions, the discovery of pastureland would have been of primary importance after a long voyage at sea.

The *Tale of the Greenlanders* contains a passage in which the word "hay" can very meaningfully be substituted for the boldfaced words representing the usual translations from the root *vin*. After describing the discovery by Tyrkir the German of **vines** and **grapes**, it goes on to say:

They slept overnight, then in the morning Leif made this announcement to his crew. "We now have two jobs to get on with, and on alternate days must **gather grapes** or **cut vines** and fell timber, so as to provide a cargo of such things for my ship." They acted upon these orders, and report has it that their tow-boat was filled with **grapes**. A full ship's cargo was cut, and in the spring they made ready and sailed away. Leif gave the land a name in accordance with the good things they found in it, calling it Vinland.[14]

The demonstration that "hay" should be read for the boldfaced words requires a few paragraphs. The first observation to be made is that the expression "**gather grapes** or **cut vines**" sounds very much like a scribe's offering of *two* interpretations of a phrase because he did not understand the exact situation. If, in fact, grapes were of some value to the Norsemen, why bother cutting vines? Why clutter their valuable cargo space with unneeded vines when they could use it for grapes instead? Several writers[15] have suggested the practical idea that vines actually were being cut for the purpose of being braided together into ersatz hawsers, or otherwise used as withes. While such a theory is indeed tempting, it must also be realized that if it were true the sagas would probably have gone into detail about the cleverness of the idea, as they did, for example, with the techniques used to catch fish. One purpose of the sagas was to record the greatness of men, and such an anecdote would almost certainly have been explained therein. Furthermore, the need for a whole boatload of such hawsers is questionable, for superior ropes of walrus hide were made at home in Greenland.

On the other hand, a towboat full of grapes (or raisins) in grape latitudes would have become nothing but a literal rot by the time of the spring sailing and could have been preserved in useful form only by their immediate fermentation into wine. However, as I have previously said, the Norsemen had no knowledge of the delicate process of fermentation of grapes. If the German Tyrkir had any such knowledge, it would certainly seem reasonable to expect to find a record of it in the sagas. Instead, he only says, "I was born where **vines and grapes** are no rarity," and nowhere do the sagas claim that anybody ever brought back wine from Vinland. Does it not make more sense that Tyrkir was simply saying that he was born where a certain kind of pasture crop was no rarity?

It can be seen from the quote above that Leif gave equal precedence ("on alternate days") to felling timber and to "**gather grapes or cut vines.**" The felling of timber may seem rather mundane compared to the preparation of noble wine, but it was of very practical importance to sailors from wood-sparse Greenland, as can be seen from Plates 1 and 2. Leif Eiriksson, in fact, received the nickname "Lucky" when he once rescued a cargo of timber. Any activity that took equal priority with the gathering of wood must have been of equal practical importance for the voyage home. I submit that because their main ship carried livestock, their towboat

was filled with hay rather than grapes. The scribe's alternate
"or cut vines" backs me up.

There is still further internal evidence that Vinland did
not produce grapes. When the Greenlanders were converted
to Christianity, they first took to it rather hesitantly, but
then wholeheartedly and even fanatically. If Vinland did
produce grapes, the Greenlanders would soon enough have
learned how to make wine for use in the sacraments, and
Vinland would have become a place of great practical importance to them well documented in written records. Instead, Vinland is mentioned only infrequently after the
Eiriksson era, and in 1237 the Greenlanders were still being
reprimanded by Rome for using beer in the sacraments.[16]

One obscure medieval manuscript, *Geographia Universalis*,
may have been close to giving the true meaning of "Vinland" when it said, "It is not very fertile except in grass and
forest." But there is further evidence of a more positive
nature that, in fact, Vinland does equal pastureland. Detailed analysis of a systematic distortion in the Yale Vinland
Map shows that the land referred to there as "Vinlanda Insula" is the same piece of land referred to by the medieval
Dutchman Jacob Cnoyen as "Grocland." What is the meaning of the word "Grocland" as used by the Dutchman
Jacob Cnoyen in place of "Vinland"? I have searched modern Dutch and middle Dutch dictionaries, modern High
German and middle High German dictionaries, plus various
dialectal dictionaries, without finding the root *groc* in any
plausible form. However, the time of Cnoyen's writing coincided with the transition between middle Dutch and modern
Dutch. It is impossible for me to say what changes in spelling were taking place during that transition, especially in
dialects. I may note, in fact, that while the famous Mercator
himself was well-versed in Dutch dialects and translated

many of Cnoyen's references into Latin, he made no attempt
to translate "Grocland" or explain its meaning. Thus, I am
forced into an intuitive kind of interpolation between middle Dutch and modern Dutch. This interpolation, however,
proves to be relatively easy. Cnoyen's root *groc* seems to
fall very nicely between the middle Dutch *crocke*, the
Flemish *krakke* and the modern Dutch *krok*, all with approximately the same meaning. The meaning?—wild pasture. So here via Cnoyen the concept of pasture again becomes associated with Vinland.

A 1508 map of Johann Ruysch seems to contain further
information about this. At an island to the west of Greenland
whose position corresponds to Cnoyen's "Grocland" and the
Yale Map's "Vinlanda," Ruysch has an obscure Latin inscription *Fei arumfeie alias cibes dicunt;* apparently a command addressed to the name of the country and ending
with the phrase, "other times they call you *cibes.*" That
these settlements were otherwise known as *cibes* is interesting, for the root *cib-* refers to fodder. However, the proper
ending *-us* for the word fodder has been replaced by *-es*.
Perhaps this is Ruysch's way of grammatically broadening
the word to mean pastureland.

But Cnoyen's "Grocland" may have had a more specific
meaning than just pastureland. In Flemish the word *krak-
keland* refers to a heath or moor, and *krakke* to heather. The
modern Dutch word *krok* generally refers to three particular species of vetch, but the middle Dutch *crocke*, used
when man was less conscious of species divisions, referred
to any vetch. The vetch is a wild legumous fodder crop having species that grow far into the Arctic. One species in
Europe has been grown for both human and animal con-
sumption since earliest times. Vetch has pods similar to peas
(vetch=wild pea), which bear varying numbers of ova de-

pending upon the species. Many species are essentially
climbing plants, having vine-like tendrils by which to at-
tach themselves to other upright plants and thus support
themselves above the ground. In fact, vetch often is found
growing among other "self-sown" cereal crops (upright
grain) in this way. Does this not sound like the description
in the sagas about the vegetation in Vinland?—wild, self-
sown grain in conjunction with some kind of vines that
bear seed clusters whose description might be mistakenly
interpreted at third hand as "grapes"? (Several writers have
raised the possibility that the self-sown grain may refer to
sandwort [*elymus arenarius*], a wild grain that was at
times used for food. Sandwort is named for its ability to
grow in apparently impossible places, and as one might
expect, it abounds in the Arctic.) There are also several
arctic species of vetch which may account for some of the
incidents described in the sagas. In the *Saga of Eirik the
Red*, after Thorhall the Hunter went off by himself, some
writers have inferred that he found grapes and ate of them,
becoming intoxicated, for he was discovered on a steep crag
where:

he lay gazing up into the air with wide-open mouth and
nostrils, scratching and pinching himself and muttering something.[17]

The corresponding situation in the *Tale of the Greenlanders*
occurs when Tyrkir the German, after being lost in the
woods and subsequently discovered by Leif and his men, is
described thus:

First he spoke for a long time in German, and rolled his eyes
many ways and twisted his mouth; but they could not make
out what he said. After a while he said in Norse: "I did not

go much farther, and yet I have a new discovery to tell of; I have found vines and grapes."[18]

It is important to note that it is not these men but all subsequent scribes and scholars who much later made whatever the original spoken words were into the written vines and grapes. And it is they who attributed both Thorhall's and Tyrkir's behavior to alcoholic intoxication. However, I think it would make more sense to rule out the unlikely possibility of instantaneous fermentation on the vine needed to produce such supposed intoxication. I would instead attribute their behavior to locoweed,[19] one of the chemically intoxicating species of vetch (*astragalus*) or its closely related[20] fellow legume *oxytropis*. The normally edible fruits of these plants take on their loco-inducing capability when barren soils, such as in the Arctic, force them to alter their mineral chemistry. Many species of *astragalus* and *oxytropis* are common deep into the Canadian Arctic,[21] and *astragalus alpinus* and *oxytropis maydelliana* are particularly abundant. *Oxytropis maydelliana* may at places become, according to Nicholas Polunin, "by far the most conspicuous plant." But why would Thorhall or Tyrkir have chosen to partake of the fruits of such plants? Perhaps they did not realize that the plants were different from the similar looking edible European vetch with which they might have been familiar. On the other hand, perhaps they did. It has been noted that animals that have been exposed to locoweed develop a craving for it.[22] Perhaps Thorhall and Tyrkir were quite intentionally "turning on."

Besides "Grocland," history has left us with one further name that may have referred to the area otherwise known as Vinland. This is the "Insula Dicolzi" of the 1448 Walsperger map and the so-called Vienna-Klosterneuberg map corpus. In the co-ordinate table of the "Nova Cosmographia" contained in the corpus,[23] this island is once referred to as "Insel Dicolzi" and another time as the "Insel Colci," so that the "Di" of Dicolzi is separable—the preposition meaning "of." Thus, the root of Dicolzi is *colzi* or *colci* (or *colzy* on the later Zeitz map.) This root has a uniform meaning in all languages that ever had any contact with Latin. It is wild cabbage—again a pasture crop. Since the Middle Ages, however, the meaning has become narrowed to a specific variety, *rape*. The rape is a fast-growing hybrid of the wild cabbage and turnip that develops individual large lower leaves forming excellent fodder and grows far into the sub-Arctic. It also bears its fruit in pods like the vetch, although it is not at all related to the vetch.

The sum of the evidence I have presented so far makes it seem likely indeed that in the minds of the original explorers of Vinland, the root *vin* referred in some way to pasture. But now it would seem that *vin* may have referred not only in general to pasture, but possibly, in this case, to some specific crop. How could it be possible for two different writers, Cnoyen with his "Grocland" and Walsperger with his "Dicolzi," to settle very specifically upon two unrelated but superficially similar fodder crops, vetch and rape, for the identification of the pasture in Vinland? One answer might be that they had access to a hypothetical, now-lost, verbal description of the vegetation, but a description that failed to specifically name the crops. Thus they would have been forced to make their own interpretations based on their individual knowledge. (In fact, the classification of plants in the pre-Linnaean Middle Ages was on a very unsure footing at best, and many of the Latin names used today have probably undergone extensive evolution from their now unknown original meanings.) It is even possible to see how the hypothesized description of the vegetation could have led to its misidentification by some writers as grapes. Aside from the fact that it bore seeds in fruit-like clusters of some sort, its leaves were also evidently described in a way that could be interpreted as referring to the broad flat leaves of the grape. As a matter of fact, the lower leaves of a mature rape plant are very similar to this description.

It would seem that the existing manuscripts of the sagas themselves reveal such an interpretative, intuitive approach by their writers.[24] That is, the background framework of that part of the sagas which deals with the vegetation is essentially a description of the characteristics of that vegetation, and the actual naming of the vegetation seems to have been superimposed upon that descriptive framework at a later time. Perhaps one can even postulate the circumstances of that superimposition. By some peculiar anomaly, the wild legumes that have been proposed as candidates for the vegetation of Vinland seem to be non-existent in Greenland.[25] Thus, when the German Tyrkir explained to the Greenlanders in the saga that he was born where vines and grapes are no rarity, he may have been merely reassuring them of his familiarity with wild legumes. But the Greenlanders would not have known a name in their own language for these unfamiliar plants, and would have been able to report about them back home only in descriptive terms or else in general terms such as "pasture." Later tellers of the sagas would be strongly tempted to replace such unwieldy descriptions by an actual species identification, correct or incorrect.

Whatever the correct identification of the vegetation in Vinland might have been, we are still left with another mystery. That is, why did all writers eventually settle *uniformly* on the incorrect identification as grapes? There are

several answers to this nagging question. First, the original
scholars who wrote down the oral sagas on parchment were
the first Norsemen to receive a formal education in the
European universities.[26] They had a solid background in
Latin and presumably studied whatever was then known
of the Latin classics. Classical Latin had already undergone
many changes to medieval Latin and the Italian languages
were already highly developed, so one can expect that their
training also involved some studies in Latin etymology. It is
known that when they returned to their homeland in the
north they turned to documenting its history. They documented it in the words of the Old Norse language, but
adapted the pen-oriented Latin alphabet to replace chisel-
oriented runes as a means of recording those words. If they
also delved into the history of their own language they may
have gotten a half-correct idea of the forgotten Old Norse
word *vin,* but their own academic background would have
tempted them to mix it up with the Latin word for grapevines.

There is even some reason to believe that a confusion between the Norse and Latin meanings may have been taking
place during the actual happening of the events described
in the sagas. If the archaic meaning of *vin* as pasture was
preserved in use until the year 1000, it could only have been
so among the farmers isolated in Iceland or Greenland.
Eirik the Red was, in fact, brought up in Iceland by his
farmer father in the midst of just such an isolated environment, and Eirik's son Leif reached maturity in Greenland
among similar conditions. They, if anybody, should have
known the true archaic Norse meaning of *vin* as pasture,
and they had no reason for misconceptions about wine. They
probably never heard the Latin word *vínum.* However, some
decades after the settlement of Greenland, a trading visit

was paid there by the young, wealthy, educated Icelander, Thorfinn Karlsefni. He was accompanied by some Norwegian trading merchants, and between them they had two ships with full crews. If these world travelers had been asked to give a meaning to the word *vin*, they probably would not have known the archaic Norse meaning, pasture. Their interpretation of the word probably would have been the Latin meaning, wine, using the long *i*.

These visitors stayed the winter in Greenland, and Leif put up the entire two crews in his spacious homestead. It is evident that Karlsefni came to know the Greenlanders well, for shortly after Christmas he took a bride: the widow of Leif's brother Thorstein. The saga tells *us* that during the winter *he* was told about Vinland, and the next spring he set out to see this land for himself and colonize it. But he did not set out with stars in his eyes, for Karlsefni's entire background was that of a shrewd businessman always attuned to profitable trade. More likely he had been informed by the Eirikssons about the true Norse meaning of Vinland. He knew that he had a good market for fodder in Greenland, for firewood anywhere in the north and a monopoly on trading if the colony succeeded.

However, the crews may not have been so informed about the meaning of *vin*. One can even imagine a shrewd master making use of and preserving the misunderstanding about wine as a means to urge his crew onward. At least one of the company seems to have been teased beyond the breaking point; namely, Thorhall the Hunter. Thorhall's country of origin is unknown, but it is known that he spent his life in activities far removed from farming. He was employed by Eirik the Red as an arctic hunter in summertime, and in wintertime to keep order among the slaves[27] and in the sprawling household. Thorhall had few friends and was de-

scribed as ill-tempered and taciturn. How could he have
been induced to leave the only man who trusted him, Eirik
the Red, and contribute his hunting talents to a three-year
expedition led by a stranger? Surely not by the idea of
finding pastureland for a group of farmer slaves with whom
his only contact was probably at the end of a staff. More
likely he had some secret dream of indulgence.

It is recorded in the saga that Thorhall began to make
trouble among the Vinland expedition soon after the first
winter set in. Food was scarce, in spite of prayers by the
new converts to Christ. Then, presumably by some hunting
trick he had learned in the north, Thorhall produced a
whale under highly dramatized circumstances, using the
occasion to declare that he had prayed to Thor instead of
Christ, and thereby alienating the entire company of Christians. Evidently Thorhall had become such a problem by
springtime that Karlsefni allowed him to assert his own
desires with regard to the further direction of the voyage:
Thorhall wanted to head homeward. Karlsefni granted him
one of the expedition's ships, but of the entire company of
160, Thorhall could only recruit a crew of nine. In those
days men did not make departing speeches or write memo-
randa for the record. Instead, they composed verses, and
Thorhall's verse tells the reader in no uncertain terms that
he felt he had been falsely led on. While preparing his ship
for sailing he was carrying water aboard. Meanwhile, he
proclaimed, in Naomi Walford's delightful translation:

> They flattered my confiding ear
> With tales of Drink abounding here:
> My curse upon the thirsty land!
> A warrior, trained to bear a brand,
> A pail instead I have to bring,

And bow my back beside the spring:
For ne'er a single draught of wine
Has passed these parching lips of mine.[28]

I must point out that this proclamation took place some six
months *after* Karlsefni's scouts discovered their cluster of
grapes and the self-sown wheat, and after Thorhall's alleged
intoxication. Evidently Thorhall and his nine recruits were
the only ones living in a dreamworld of wine, and his
parting verse gives a glimpse of the reality of Vinland:

Now let the vessel plow the main
To Greenland and our friends again:
Away, and leave the strenuous host
Who praise this God-forsaken coast
To linger in a desert land,
And boil their whales in Furdustrand.[29]

Perhaps even if someone had tried to explain to Thorhall
that Vinland really meant pastureland, he still would have
preferred to continue believing it meant wineland. He may
have provided one of the first examples of the most important factor in the change of *Vinland* to *Vínland*. That factor
is self-deception.

Self-deception was one of the most highly developed arts
of the Middle Ages. The extent to which religion and theol-
ogy were applied as tools in this art is well known, and with
the first breaths of the development of modern science,
alchemy and astrology came to be employed toward the
same end. Even history was employed toward the end of
self-deception, and the existence of the Roman Empire was
maintained on paper and in form many centuries after its
actual practical death. One of the more cherished self-de-

ceptions, especially after it was realized that the classical glory of the ancient world had passed completely away and the Second Coming of Christ had still not occurred, was the idea of an earthly paradise.

One of the more popular beliefs in an earthly paradise was that in the *Insulae Fortunatae*, or Isles of the Blessed. Perhaps based on an actual ancient knowledge of the Canaries or Azores by the Phoenicians and Carthaginians, this belief told of an archipelago far out in the ocean toward the setting sun where grapes and self-sown wheat grew in abundance, which was supposedly to be discovered and inhabited by all manner of saintly people. Nansen has noted many striking analogies between the Vinland stories and the stories of the *Insulae Fortunatae*, and has drawn particular attention to one such Irish myth—the story of Saint Brandan —that could well have influenced the interpretation of the original Vinland stories. Irish-Norse contact was well established, and the Irish myth of Saint Brandan's search for the earthly paradise, which was written down on paper sometime during the Vinland era, was well known verbally in Iceland. Nansen summarizes it:

In the Latin *Navigatio Sancti Brandani*, a description of Brandan's seven-years sea-voyage in search of the Promised Land, it is related that one day a mighty bird came flying to Brandan and the brethren who were with him in the coracle [an Irish ship[30]]; it had a branch in its beak with a bunch of grapes of unexampled size and redness, and it dropped the branch into the lap of the man of God. The grapes were as large as apples and they lived on them for twelve days.

Three days afterward they reached the island: it was covered with the thickest forest of vines, which bore grapes with such incredible fertility that all the trees were bent to the earth; all

with the same fruit and the same color; not a tree was unfruit-
ful; and there were none found there of any other sort.

Then this man of God goes ashore and explores the island,
while the brethren wait in the boat (like Karlsefni and his men
waiting for the runners) until he comes back to them bringing
samples of the fruits of the island (as the runners brought with
them samples of the product of Wineland). He says, "Come
ashore and set up the tent, and regale yourself with the excellent
fruits of this land, which the Lord has shown us." For forty days
they lived well on the grapes, and when they left they loaded the
boat with as many of them as it would hold, (exactly like Leif
in the *Tale of the Greenlanders*) . . .[31]

Nansen, as interpreted by some of his readers, contended
that stories such as this formed the *entire* basis for the Vinland sagas and that there was no actual historic event behind them. In this case, he surely would have been wrong,
but he undoubtedly was right that a story like that of St.
Brandan's Blessed Isle would help muddle attempts at a
valid description of Vinland.[32] In particular, one cannot
help but be struck by the importance of grapes in impressing
the medieval European mind with the fertility of a place. A
Greenland farmer unfamiliar with grapes may not have appreciated this importance, but an Adam of Bremen or an
educated saga composer in Iceland would have. The Greenland farmer might well have appreciated the play on words
between *vin* and *vín* when it was explained to him, however, and endorsed the importance of grapes when he heard
it suggested. Such a play on words would have even been
enhanced by the apparent imprecision of the original word
vin in its possible interpretation, besides pasture, as "a good
place to settle in,"[33] as would have been the Isles of the
Blessed.

Regardless of these speculations, one point can be stated

with certainty. That is, if the original, now lost, oral Greenland versions of the sagas did in fact say "Vinland" with a
short *i* meaning pasture, they still would have been changed
upon their telling in Iceland in later centuries, inevitably
and inexorably, to accented long *i* sounds meaning wineland. For, without the long *i* the word had no meaning at
all to the more cosmopolitan people of Iceland, who had
long since forgotten *vin*=pasture. Their only available conclusion was that the Greenlanders must have been mis-pro-
nouncing *vín*=wine, a word with which their closer ties
to Europe had familiarized them. Once it was recognized,
however, that such "corrections" had to be made to the
pronunciation (or, later, the spelling) of key words of the
saga, the gate would have been opened for changes in the
description of the vegetation as well. Thus, the conclusion
that seems inescapable is that the oral sagas as they had
been known in early Greenland referred to Vinland as pastureland, but the written or oral sagas in Iceland—perhaps
just as early—referred to it as a land of wine. Since all the
existing manuscripts have come from Iceland, we can have
no hope of seeing in them any trace of *vin*=pasture.

But I do conclude that Vinland originally did refer to
pastureland. When one gives up the romantic interpretation of Vinland as "wineland" and accepts the realistic interpretation as "pastureland," then an entirely new range of
possibilities for its location in the northern latitudes is
opened up.

CHAPTER 4

The Norse Story in Saga and Stone

The primary hope for locating Vinland has always been in the sailing directions in the sagas. Indeed, in the case of Vinland the sagas give *so much* in the way of detailed sailing directions that it almost seems impossible for any actual location to satisfy the dictates of all of them. Entire books have been devoted to rationalizing away apparent contradictions in the directions and interpreting them in preferred ways, with the intent of proving that Vinland must have been some particular place or another. The various arguments have proved more about the power of rationalization than about the location of Vinland.[1] Thus, it would seem that a very important rule to adopt would be to let the sagas speak entirely for themselves on the subject, with no interpretation. If a location for Vinland can be found that fits the words of the saga the way they are written, then the probability that this location actually represents Vinland seems high—indeed, higher than that of a location that requires explanation and interpretation of the words in the sagas, however valid or true the explanation might be. Unfortunately, in applying this criterion to my

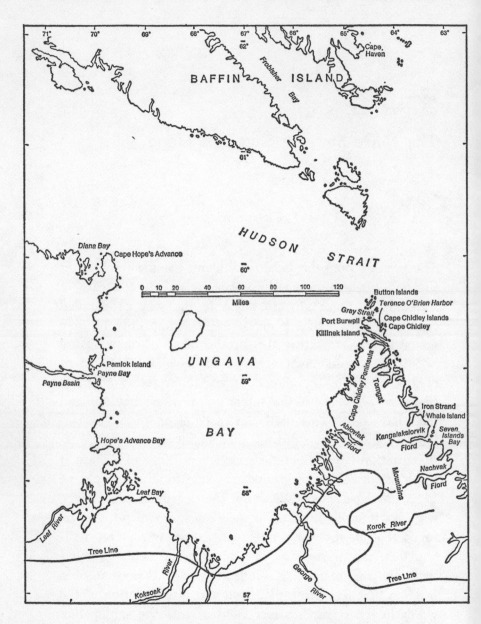

The setting of the Vinland scenario.

1.   Eirik the Red's farm near the southern tip of Greenland. According to Norse sagas, Leif Eiriksson's voyage to Vinland in America started from here. The medieval Norse settlements were located near the modern Greenland towns of Godthaab and Julianehaab, shown on the endpaper maps inside this book's covers.

2.   Modern Greenland village built with stones from the ruins of the Norsemen's cathedral. The fields adjacent to the cathedral have the richest soil in all Greenland, but the Greenland landscape has practically no trees.

3, 4. Occasional forest oases, far above the tree line in the middle of the arctic tundra, are found all the way from Siberia (*above*) across Canada to Baffin Island (*right*). Leif Eiriksson's Vinland, previously thought to have been a temperate land of wild grapes, may have actually been a more arctic-like land of pastures such as the one shown here, discussed in Chapter 3.

5. The sagas' "Markland," according to Chapter 2, was *not* the towering forest of Labrador as heretofore theorized, but instead a nearly arctic land composed of unusual woody scrub growths of hybrid willows like these.

6. The mile-thick icecap of Greenland pushes right down to the ocean. It restricted the Norse settlements to a narrow coastal band and forced Norse sailors constantly to dodge the icebergs calved off by it.

7. Currents drifting southward from the polar sea carry year-round pack ice which blockaded the Greenland east coast to Norse ships. Elsewhere in the Arctic, pack ice, frozen solid on the sea itself in winter, breaks up into floes in spring and disappears in summer. Thus, in summer the Norsemen were free to sail all about the Arctic. This geography is clarified on the endpaper maps.

8. Archaeological artifacts proving that the southward explorations reported in the sagas were also supplemented by unreported *northward* explorations. These Norse objects, ranging from an iron hammer to a "spinning wheel" spindle weight, were found in Eskimo ruins a thousand miles north of the tip of Greenland. They prove that Norsemen traded peaceably with the Eskimos rather than warring with them, as discussed in Chapter 7.

9. Traces of Norsemen at an Eskimo ruin 1500 miles north of the settlements, at the northwesternmost corner of Greenland. In the center are a rusted fragment of chain-mail armor, a spearhead and two chessmen. The chessmen suggest that the Norse presence in northwesternmost Greenland was at least sufficiently permanently established to include leisure-time activities.

own thinking, I find that I am *not able* to find a location in Baffin Island that satisfies the sailing directions to Vinland. Thus, adherence to this criterion requires that I rule out the numerically tempting idea of Chapter 2 that the three prominences of Baffin Island were the three lands of the sagas.

However, I shall describe a candidate location for Vinland just across Hudson Strait in mainland Canada, along the west shore of Ungava Bay of northern Quebec. I believe this area does offer some probability of yielding the actual site of Leif's houses which he built at Vinland. This theory rests heavily upon the seemingly fair statement in the *Saga of Eirik the Red* that Thorfinn Karlsefni never did find Leif's house in Vinland but, rather, sailed up and down some wrong coastline looking for it. Although the Greenlanders' Tale states that Karlsefni reached Leif's house all safe and sound, Edward Reman has shown that Eirik's Saga is the one that should be trusted when dealing with Karlsefni.[2] My own hypothetical scenario, which I propose to compare with a literal reading of the sagas, may be followed on the adjacent map. The scenario follows:

The Eirikssons found Helluland and Markland on one or another of the promontories of Baffin Island and somehow missed or ignored the third promontory of Baffin on their voyages southward. They then encountered the north-pointing Cape Chidley Peninsula of northernmost Labrador, partly as a result of tidal currents which headed them into Hudson Strait. These five-knot currents, capable of overwhelming sailboats, are well known to arctic navigators,[3] and probably constituted the first Norse experience with what were later to become known as "in-drawing channels."[4]

The Eirikssons sailed west across Ungava Bay and on the

west shore, perhaps in the neighborhood of Payne or Leaf
Bay, built Leif's house. On a later expedition, Leif's brother
Thorvald explored south along the west shore of Ungava
Bay, eastward along its southern shore, then northward
along the Cape Chidley Peninsula. Somewhere around the
tip of this peninsula Thorvald repaired his keel and named a
place Kjalarnes.

When Karlsefni came looking for these places with a load
of hopeful colonists, he had the misfortune of unknowingly
sailing past them during the outgoing tide, thereby missing
the opening to Hudson Strait. Thus, he ended up searching
up and down the east coast of the Cape Chidley Peninsula,
mistaking it for the similarly oriented Ungava coastline
which was actually some five degrees westward. Karlsefni
made some attempts to find Leif's houses along this incorrectly identified coast, but the presence of the large number of would-be colonists made it imperative to concentrate
on setting up winter quarters before exploring extensively.
Thorhall the Hunter, who perhaps had been along on the
Eiriksson expeditions, knew that the proper way to Leif's
house was north to the opening of Hudson Strait, then
westward. Karlsefni later did explore the entrance into Hudson Strait, but stayed along the east shore of Ungava Bay
without crossing it, and thus missed Leif's house again.

The first question that must be asked about this hypothesis is whether there is a place on the west coast of Ungava
Bay which it would be reasonable to call Vinland, with the
meaning of pastureland that I have already shown. The
answer has in fact already been given, unawares, by many
people who have visited this area and described it. The
chief authority on the vegetation of the eastern Canadian
Arctic, Nicholas Polunin, spares himself writing his own de-

scription of Payne Bay's vegetation but rather quotes somebody else's description of even more northerly Diana Bay
as wholly applicable also to Payne Bay:

. . . of all the many hundreds of miles I have travelled in the
Arctic, I have not yet met the place so rich in lichen as this.
The meadows stretch for acres uninterrupted by rock, and
clothed with deep rich lichen with the usual grass growing up
between. There is mile upon mile of them—dry, rich sandy soil
clothed with moss and lichen. The richness and abundance of
the lichen more than the moss is simply wonderful; a reindeer
herd would go for years here without want.[5]

Polunin also refers to some protected places in this vicinity
where leaves remain green all winter. His use of the word
"meadow" is particularly striking indeed, and Polunin uses
it several times in describing areas on the west of Ungava
Bay. Without a doubt, Leif Eiriksson could have found
places here deserving of the name "Vinland," with a short
i. He might have been just as likely to use the word
"meadow" in describing the area as the modern explorers.
Another such is V. Tanner, who makes these general comments about northernmost Labrador's vegetation:

In some spots on slight slopes a meadow-like vegetation is to be
found forming, so to say, oases in the mountain tundra. . . . At
the most protected heads of the many lakes yellowish-green,
meadow-like areas are to be found, at lower elevations with
willow patches and occasional thickets of alder. . . . On flat
bottoms in river valleys and on their deltas, the alluvial plains,
especially the large ones, are almost covered by meadows with
Juncus, Eriophorum, Carices and grasses up to 50 cm. [½ yd.]
high.[6]

Such oases in the Ungava area have been dubbed the
"arctic prairies,"[7] and agricultural experiments have shown

that with proper fertilization these Ungava soils will even yield garden vegetables.[8] For those who still insist on some kind of "wine-berry" in Vinland, the Ungava Eskimos have been known to collect a naturally growing edible berry,[9] but in any case, there is plenty of summer pasture.[10]

If the suggestion of a semi-arctic Vinland still seems radical to some, they are referred to Vilhjalmur Stefansson's survey of the modern awakening to the true nature of summer in the Arctic.[11] Actually, I have been preceded in my interpretation by at least one writer, Edward Reman, who in a slightly different setting has given many convincing arguments that the sagas do describe a sub-arctic location for Vinland.[12] Another writer, Paul Adam, concludes, after a study of Norse sailing capabilities, that it is quite impossible to sustain any interpretation of the sailing times and directions of the sagas which place Vinland in more southerly areas.[13] He does, however, find the conditions quite compatible with the placement of Vinland in the Ungava Bay area, as I do.

The best test of the validity of my above hypothetical scenario in the Ungava Bay area is to use it as a backdrop for a re-enactment of the actual sailing directions of the sagas. I will endeavor to demonstrate a jigsaw fit, point by point, of every geographical description in the sagas with a real place on the map accompanying the scenario. Obviously, this will entail the mentioning of many place names whose importance to the discussion is only local and need not be remembered.

The following extracts from the sagas are generally based on Gwyn Jones's translations in his *Norse Atlantic Saga,* but occasionally my own translations supersede his. The extracts are given with my proposed identification of places italicized in brackets, and a casual reader may skip these italics entirely. But, in the event that he may occasionally desire to check where these places are, he should keep a marker at the scenario map on page 50 during this extended discussion:

From there [Markland] they [Leif's original expedition] now sailed out to sea and were at sea two days before catching sight of land [*Cape Chidley Peninsula*]. They sailed to land, reaching an island which lay north of it [*Button Islands*], where they went ashore and looked around them in fine weather, and found that there was dew on the grass, whereupon it happened to them that they set their hands to the dew, then carried it to their mouths, and thought they had never known anything so sweet as that was.

Mariners frequently refer to fresh water as "sweet" water, and if Leif's expedition had run low on this commodity while at sea in fine weather, they would not have been able to replenish it. Of the summer sub-arctic dews, Tanner says: ". . . low humidity occurs during the day and a high percentage of humidity after the rapid cooling by radiation during the night, resulting on clear nights in the formation of abundant dew. Close to the seashore very heavy dew falls; the walls of the tent do not dry till the afternoon if the weather is calm, and pools of water remain on the tarpaulins the whole day."[14] The two-day thirst implied in the above saga quotation would have been a good reason for Leif's stopping immediately at the first islands he came to, the Button Islands, before even going to the mainland, on the scenario map, behind them.

After which they returned to their ship and sailed into the sound [*Gray Strait*] which lay between the island and the cape projecting north from the land itself [*Cape Chidley Peninsula*].

They made headway west round the cape [*across Ungava Bay*]. There were big shallows there [*west coast of Ungava Bay*] at low water; their ship went aground, and it was a long way to look to get sight of the sea from the ship.

Concerning the west coast of Ungava Bay the *Arctic Pilot* says, "From Leaf River to Hope's Advance Bay, 30 miles north-westward, innumerable islands of all sizes so mask this stretch of coast that it is impossible to distinguish the mainland. . . . From Hope's Advance Bay to Payne Bay, a distance of 40 miles, the coast is fronted by islands and shallow water, extending 10 miles from it, no landing being obtainable excepting on the outer islands. . . . The coast from Payne Bay runs almost due north for about 65 miles in form of a slight bay to Cape Hope's Advance. The coast is low and broken into numerous wide, shallow bays, which at low water show great expanses of boulder-strewn flats. . . . For 20 miles northward of Payne River the coast is fringed with rocky islands. . . . The water between these islands is so shallow that they are practically joined to the mainland, and to one another when the tide is low. Outside the islands, the water continues shallow for a considerable distance."[15]

But they were so curious to get ashore they had no mind to wait for the tide to rise under their ship, but went hurrying off to land where a river flowed out of a lake [*Payne River and Basin* (60° N.) *or Leaf River and Lake* (59° N.)].

Six and a half miles inland from the mouth of the Payne estuary on the scenario map, the river mouth broadens out into a wide channel called Payne Basin, which Leif may have thought of as a lake. Otherwise, a reasonable candidate for this identification might be Leaf River and Leaf Lake or Basin.

Then as soon as the tide rose under their ship, they took their boat, rowed back to her, and brought her up into the river, and so to the lake, where they cast anchor, carried their skin sleeping bags off-board and built themselves huts. [This spot, wherever it was, was later to receive the name Vinland.] Later they decided to winter there and built a big house. . . . Day and night were of a more equal length there than in Greenland or Iceland. On the shortest day of winter the sun was visible at 3:00 P.M. as well as at 9:00 A.M. [*thus, latitude 59° N., approximately*].

In that era, of course, there was no clock time, and the actual Norse times named, *eyktarstadr* and *dagmálastadr*, are nowadays imperfectly understood.[16] The translated times I have adopted here are the modern Icelandic interpretations of those times, arrived at through some unknown process in the past when Christianity introduced Iceland to clock time. However, since Torfaeus in 1705, scholars in the "wine-land" camp have sought to force a rationalized interpretation of the times more in line with grape latitudes.[17] Such rationalization is no longer acceptable unless it can stand on its own evidence, which has not been adequately offered. In any case, the unequivocal statement that day and night were more equal in Vinland than in Greenland requires something south of Greenland's southern tip at 60°, and lends weight to the candidacy of Leaf Lake over Payne Bay for Vinland. (However, this requirement might be eliminated by noting that the Eiriksson farmstead in Greenland was actually above 61°.) In fact, just how accurately the Norsemen could have measured sunrise and sunset times is unknown.

The next set of sailing directions is in the description of

the voyage of Leif's brother Thorvald and of his stay at
Leif's house in Vinland:

But in the spring Thorvald ordered them to make their ship
ready, and for the ship's boat and certain of the men to proceed
along the west coast [*of Ungava Bay*] and explore there during
the summer. They saw that that land was fair and wooded* with
a short distance between the wood and the sea and white sands.
It was very full of islands and great shallows [regarding this, see
the above quotation from the *Arctic Pilot*]. . . . Next summer
Thorvald [and the entire expedition] set off eastward [*along
the south shore of Ungava Bay*] with the merchant-ship and
further north along the land [*along Cape Chidley Peninsula*].
Off a certain cape [*the northwest corner of Killinek Island,
near Port Burwell?*] they met with heavy weather, were driven
ashore and broke the keel from under the ship. . . . Thorvald
said to his shipmates, "I should like to erect the [old, broken
and now replaced] keel on the cape here and call it Kjalarnes
(Ness of the Keel)." This they did, and afterward sailed away
and east along the land [*through Gray Strait*], and into the
mouth of the next fiord they came to [*Sir Terence O'Brien
harbor behind the Cape Chidley Islands*], and to a headland
jutting out there which was all grown with wood. They brought
the ship to where they could moor her, thrust out a gangway to
the shore, and Thorvald walked ashore with the full ship's company. "This is a fair place," he said, "and here I should like to
build my farmstead."

To most southern people, the low-lying lands Thorvald
had previously been visiting would seem more attractive
than a walled fiord, but it must be remembered that Thorvald was a Greenlander and accustomed to fiord living. For
two preceding years he had seen nothing but the low coast-
lines surrounding Ungava Bay, and the fiord behind Cape

---

* The manuscript does *not* say "well" wooded, as some translators
have attempted to make it do.

Chidley Islands on the scenario map is the first true fiord he could have seen. Of this, the *Arctic Pilot* says, ". . . it is landlocked, has 12 and 13 fathoms all the way in through a narrow pass, with 9 fathoms in the anchorage; the only trouble being that the place is very squally, the cliffs rising abruptly all round from 1000 to 1500 feet, the squalls come down from them with terrible force; the holding ground is, however, good. The harbor is used by fishermen, and is said to be safe and good in all weathers."[18] While these gusts may seem forbidding to a southerner, someone used to the *föhn* storms off the Greenland glacier could have merely considered them as small reminders of home.

Here, after an encounter with natives, Thorvald lost his life and was buried on the headland, which now received the name Krossanes (Ness of the Cross). The only remaining other voyage about which course descriptions were recorded was Karlsefni's unsuccessful attempt to colonize Vinland, as told in the *Saga of Eirik the Red:*

Then when two days were past [after having left Markland] they sighted land [*Cape Chidley Peninsula*], and sailed to the land. Where they arrived there was a cape [*Cape Chidley*]. They beat along the coast and left the land to starboard [*thus sailing down the Labrador coast and missing the entrance to Hudson Strait and Ungava Bay*]. There were long beaches and sands there [*Iron Strand, at 59°30′ N.*]. They put ashore in boats and came across the keel of a ship on a ness, so called the place Kjalarnes.

This was probably not, however, the same keel which Thorvald left along the shore of Ungava Bay, but that of some unfortunate Atlantic-tossed wreck. Karlsefni was lost, and apparently willing to delude himself into thinking this was Thorvald's Kjalarnes.

Likewise they gave a name to the beaches and called them
Furdustrandir ["Awesome strands"] because it was so long sailing past them.

The *Labrador and Hudson Bay Pilot* says about this spot on
the scenario map, "Iron Strand is a stretch of black, sandy
beach that extends about 6 miles northwestward from
Murphy Head to the Helga River."[19] Probably the fore-
boding darkness of the sand as well as its extent contributed
to the choice of the name "Awesome strands." The sagas
have elsewhere described sands as white whenever possible,
but here that adjective is conspicuously missing.

Then the coast became invaginated, and toward this inlet they
headed their ship. . . . They sailed the ship up into this fiord
[*Kangalaksiorvik Fiord at* 59°25' *N.*] off whose mouth lay an
island [*the islands of Seven Islands Bay*].

The manuscript later uses the plural in referring to the
islands at the mouth of the fiord, but here is concentrating
on a particular one about to receive a name.

There were prominent currents at this island, so they called it
Straumey [*perhaps present-day Whale Island*].

The description of these currents in the saga may be explained by the fact that in the area under consideration on
the scenario map, offshore of Seven Islands Bay, there exists
an extensive shoal which would divert part of the Labrador Current during peak seasons into the deeper waters of
Seven Islands Bay, filling it with eddies.

There were so many birds there that a man could hardly set
foot down between the eggs. They held on into the fiord, and

called it Straumsfjord [*present Kangalaksiorvik Fiord*]. Here they carried their goods off the ships and made their preparations.

This expedition had come with the specific intent of founding a colony and could not afford to spend time looking for Leif's houses without building their own. There were too many people to live aboard the ship continuously.

They had brought all sorts of livestock with them, and looked around at what the land had to offer. There were mountains there, and the prospect round was beautiful [*Torngat Mountains*].

Concerning this view, Wilfred Grenfell says, ". . . the Torngats afford the most lofty land immediately adjacent to the coast in all the long stretch from Baffin Land to Cape Horn. . . . in all eastern America there is no scenery that even approaches in scale and ruggedness the Torngats."[20]

They paid no heed to anything save exploring the country. There was abundant grass there. They spent the winter there, and a hard winter it proved with no provision made for it. They were in a bad way for food, and the hunting and fishing failed. . . . In the spring they went up into Straumsfjord and got supplies from every source, hunting on the mainland, eggs in the breeding grounds and fishing from the sea.

Now they talked over their expedition and made plans. Thorhall the Hunter wished to proceed north above Furdustrandir to search for Vinland, but Karlsefni wished to travel south along the land.

That is, Thorhall knew that Karlsefni had missed the turn off into Hudson Strait; Thorhall wanted to find this and head westward. In spite of his nasty reputation, Thorhall must have had some significant abilities to merit the trust

Eirik the Red put in him. Meanwhile, the world trader and
navigator Karlsefni must have known the solar observations
to expect at Leif's house, and knew that his present location
was not quite far enough south.

So now Thorhall began making ready out by the islands [of
which Straumey was one] . . . Afterwards they [Thorhall and
his crew] sailed northward beyond Furdustrandir and Kjalarnes
and wanted to beat to westward. They met with a storm and
were shipwrecked. . . . Karlsefni sailed south along the land
[evidently leaving some of the colonists behind at Straumsfjord,
however]. . . . They journeyed at length as far as to where a
river flowed down from the land into a lake, and then to the sea
[*via Nachvak Fiord at 59°4' N.*].

Karlsefni was looking for a place that answered the geographical description of Leif's Vinland with its lake and
river, and the first place that had these characteristics was
indeed a good candidate. Of course, this search could easily
become a time-consuming process, as the head of every
fiord had to be investigated.

Prominent sand-spits off the mouth of the river prevented their
entering it except at high flood tide.

This difficulty of approach, according to Leif's description,
is another characteristic which Vinland was supposed to
have. But the effect of these sandspits on Karlsefni's progress
was evidently minor in comparison with the previously
quoted effect experienced by Leif when his ship was
grounded, for immediately:

Karlsefni sailed into it and called the place Hop (meaning
Landlocked Bay).

This place on the scenario map was, I propose, Tasiuyak
Arm, the northern arm at the head of Nachvak Fiord,
59° 4′ N. Of this almost landlocked arm the *Labrador and
Hudson Bay Pilot* says, "Townley Head, the northern face of
Kityaupak Mountain, is a bluff separating Tallek Arm from
Tasiuyak Arm, the inner end of Nachvak Fiord. The northwestern extremity of Townley Head terminates in a spit that
dries and narrows the fiord to less than a quarter of a
mile."[21] This description seems to fit very well William
Hovgaard's illustration of the Old Norse technical word
"hop."[22] There is, in fact, a river that flows through this
arm and across this narrow mouth, which then, with a
thousand years less of the river's erosion, may have been
shallower than the present fifteen fathoms. Karlsefni would
have noted the fact that this physical description of these
surroundings fitted Leif's portrait of Vinland. Karlsefni
may also have found interest in the solar observations here
at Nachvak Fiord, for the latitude is essentially the same
as at Leaf Basin on the proposed true Vinland coast of
Ungava Bay.

. . . They now spent the winter there. Not a bit of snow came,
and the stock was able to feed itself outdoors.

This seems most clearly and importantly a reference to a
low precipitation level in the area rather than to the
temperature. As an example of a similar phenomenon, the
weather station at Arctic Bay in northernmost Baffin Island
records an average total annual precipitation of less than
seven inches.[23] Extremely dry winters have been encountered in several arctic localities, and occasionally whatever
snow might have fallen is blown completely away by strong
winds.[24] As previously remarked, the mosses and lichens

thus left exposed form very good grazing meadows. Modern Greenlanders frequently leave their sheep out all winter long if the snow is not too deep.

. . . And now Karlsefni and his followers returned to Straumsfjord. It is some men's report that Bjarni and Freydis [other leaders in the expedition] had remained behind there, and a hundred men with them, and proceeded no further, while Karlsefni and Snorri had travelled south with forty men, yet spent no longer at Hop than a bare two months, and got back again that same summer. Then Karlsefni set off with one ship to look for Thorhall the Hunter, while the rest of the party stayed behind. They went north past Kjalarnes, and then bore away west, with the land on their port side [*through Gray Strait, then down along the west coast of the Cape Chidley Peninsula*]. There was a desolate wilderness to be seen ahead with almost nowhere a clearing therein.

This may or may not have been a glimpse at the coniferous tree line that approaches Ungava Bay in the interior of the Cape Chidley Peninsula. The statement is too general to differentiate between this and the taiga scrub thickets, which become infestations as one goes southward.[25]

And when they had travelled at length, a river fell down out of the land from east to west [*Abloviak Fiord at 59°30' N. or Korok River at 58°50' N.*].

Some translators interpret the text to say the river flowed from southeast to northwest. In this case the river would be the George River, whose mouth almost coincides with the Korok. If they had sailed up the George they surely would have seen the tree line.

They put into this river mouth and lay at anchor off the southern bank. . . . Then they moved away and back north. . . . They decided that the mountains which they had seen at Hop [*Torn-gat Mountains*] were the very same mountains as those which they now found, and they concluded that the distance either way from Straumsfjord was about the same.

This mind-boggling comparison is clarified by the scenario map. Namely, the Torngat Mountains reach their greatest height around Nachvak Fiord and Kangalaksiorvik Fiord, and are quite impressive from the Atlantic side of the Cape Chidley Peninsula. From the Ungava Bay side one can occasionally see these very same mountains on the eastern horizon, out over the low-lying lands of the Ungava Bay coast. The *Arctic Pilot* says, "The mouth of the Koksoak River is situated 155 miles south-westward from the western entrance to Gray Strait. In ordinary weather the high land of the Labrador shore may be seen towering above the scarcely discernible coast of Ungava Bay, while traversing the first sixty or seventy miles of the course, after which little is seen till near Koksoak River."[26] Abloviak Fiord is within this sixty or seventy miles, but the Korok and George rivers are not. Nevertheless, the saga implies that the expedition went back north before seeing the mountains.

This completes the extended comparison of my hypothetical scenario with the detailed passages of the sagas containing sailing directions. Is the correspondence satisfactory? If there is to be complete confidence in the proposed location of Vinland on the west coast of Ungava Bay, then one must investigate all possible discrepancies thoroughly. While many features of the proposed scenario fit the above sailing directions quite well, there are nevertheless some places where the fit is not quite so comfortable. At least one descriptive quote can be cited from the sagas which is completely incompatible with the characteristics of the area of my hypothetical scenario. According to the *Tale of the Greenlanders'* description of Leif's Vinland, "No frost came during the winter, and the grass hardly withered." This statement leaves no room for interpretation in terms of precipitation level and simply states that the temperature was above 32° F. all winter long. However, I believe it is the only statement in all the sagas implying a sub-tropical location for Vinland. In fact, *none* of the seriously proposed theories of the location of Vinland have been able to satisfy this statement, and to do so one would have to postulate a Vinland nearly in Florida. Nevertheless, I am not yet willing to reject this statement as spurious, but will just leave it as an unanswered problem. A clue toward an eventual answer might be forthcoming from Polunin's observation of places in northern Quebec where leaves remained green all winter through.[27]

While it is true that the location of Vinland proposed here satisfies more points of description in the sagas than any of the many others proposed, complete confidence in it requires still an additional test. Even if one were to arrive at a geographical theory that could be reconciled with every last detail in the sagas, there would still be a major question left unanswered. That is, do the sagas as we know them faithfully reflect the Vinland of Leif Eiriksson, or were the sailing directions in them later edited to conform with varying current theory on its location? The possibility of such variance is inherent in the very existence of many differing Vinland maps, and there easily may have been other, now lost variants of the sagas. In fact, the very presence of such detailed sailing directions in the sagas may be more a reflection of later concern with finding Vinland than early generosity of information.

The ultimate proof of the location of Vinland will, of course, have to depend on unequivocal archaeological evidence. In this regard, there are at least six sites referred to in the sagas where archaeological remains might be sought: Karlsefni's houses at Hop, the houses at Straumsfjord, Thorvald's grave at Krossanes, Leif's house at Vinland, Leif's "booths" (temporary huts) at Vinland and a house built at Vinland by a certain Helgi and Finnbogi who accompanied a separate, infamous voyage not discussed here of Freydis, Eirik's daughter. In addition to these there may be other unrecorded candidate sites, for example some probably built when a certain Bishop Gnuppsson went searching for Vinland a century after Leif Eiriksson. Thus, it is quite reasonable to hope for the discovery of archaeological remains.

However, not just any Norse ruins will constitute a proof that a given area truly was Vinland. One must consider possible constructions and even communities associated with shipwrecks which had nothing at all to do with Vinland. If any archaeological evidence is to be unequivocally valid, it must depend on more than mere carbon dating approximately to the Vinland era. Some discovery must be made that bears the clear stamp of Leif Eiriksson or Vinland and could not have been produced by any other Norse agency. This latter requirement even rules out any evidence supplied by mere rune stones bearing, say, the name Vinland, for many people thought later that they were in Vinland when they were at many different places. (To cite an analogy, a known 1347 voyage to "Markland" was undoubtedly to the towering forests of Ungava-Labrador and not to the true original Markland, wherever it was.[28])

There is one archaeological site associated with the Vinland expeditions that avoids many of the problems previously mentioned. That is the grave of Thorvald Eiriksson at Krossanes. The materials put into a grave are usually selected specifically to withstand great periods of time and, simultaneously, are frequently either selected to, or incidentally happen to, convey much information about the dead man. The locating of this particular grave may indeed prove more important archaeologically than locating Leif's house in Vinland, and certainly should receive much more attention from scholars than it has. A fitting observation of the millennial anniversary of Vinland would be to honor an unfulfilled wish of Thorstein Eiriksson to bring the remains of his brother Thorvald back to the recently rediscovered Eiriksson family graveyard in Brattahlid, Greenland.[29]

Of course, one place where there would be only slight probability of archaeological contamination by Atlantic castaways is the west shore of Ungava Bay. This shore is shielded from all castaways except those that would happen to enter Hudson Strait during an incoming tide. If Norse ruins dating from the Vinland era were to be found there, the probability would be high that they had some actual connection with Leif's Vinland.

In fact, some very curious ruins have been found along the Ungava shore I have been discussing, including some right at the mouth of Payne Bay. I have not been able to examine these ruins personally, but I find the published reports most interesting. The Canadian anthropologist Thomas E. Lee has explored both extensively and intensively in this region, almost annually, and has concluded that the ruins are inescapably Norse.

The most difficult problem to be faced, when the relative importance of the various candidate sites is agreed upon, is the decision as to whether or not to excavate at all, and if so, how to go about it. There is only one site in the world that actually contains Leif's house, and once it is excavated the job cannot be redone again later. In this kind of excavation one would be looking for much more than mere cultural indicators such as spindle whorls, rune stones and similar weather-resistant items. To expect an unequivocal Vinland or Eirikssonian stamp one would need to depend on much more perishable evidence such as wooden rune sticks or tablets, embroidered cloth or similar manuscript-like data. But the nearest one could hope to come to perishable remains in Vinland would be to find their insoluable chemical traces in the soil.

The current state of the art of archaeological techniques is simply not capable of this kind of detective work. Until the development of radio-carbon dating within recent decades, the primary tool of the archaeologist, aside from his sharp mind, has been the crude shovel or trowel. However, another tool, which may someday permit on-the-spot mapping of chemical traces in the soil, is the gas chromatographic analyzer combined with the mass spectrometer. While still primarily a laboratory device, portable forms of this tool are being produced. Similar advances in nuclear magnetic resonance spectrometry, neutron activation and other techniques yet unknown may appear at any time. And a major break-through in the combination of computers with various analytical instruments appears to be in store for this decade or the next. Indeed, the very practice of archaeology is coming more and more to be the handling of large amounts of detailed statistical data and will certainly be revolutionized in the near future by the computer.

So, given the doubt about what results present limited techniques would produce, a question that must be answered by any archaeologist when something is found is whether or not to dig at all right now. Another decade in the soil will not harm something already buried a thousand years, whereas hasty excavation certainly might. Delay would also

allow for the proper major discussion and planning necessary before such a project. The question might well be
asked, "But what would one expect to find, even if such
techniques did become available?" If the nineteenth-century treasure hunters who pilfered countless ruins before
archaeology became a science had asked that question of
someone who suggested more painstaking techniques, he
would have been unable to answer. But the ground surely
contains more than meets the naked eye. How many archaeologists who made excavations a few decades ago without the use of carbon dating wish they had waited until
now? The answer is, probably, not many. Careers have to
be built, and they cannot be built by waiting. The individual is in no position to restrain himself from destroying
potential future gains for others when there is possible present gain for himself. This is realistic and, indeed, proper.
Only larger groups such as professional societies and gov-
ernments can hope to have the huge detachment necessary
to make such decisions. Hopefully, such bodies will take an
active interest in the sites in Ungava.

Thomas Lee, in fact, has already completely excavated
some of the ruins found along Ungava Bay, those located
on tiny Pamiok Island at the mouth of Payne Bay.[30] For the
present, the most important question about these Norse
house ruins at the mouth of Payne Bay is whether they were
built during the Vinland era. In answer to this, matter
from the oldest floor of one house was carbon dated at
A.D. 1050.[31]

The exposed location of Pamiok Island does not seem to
fit the saga description of Leif's lake-bound Vinland, and
these remains are probably not Leif's own houses. However, it is known from the sagas that other travelers to
Vinland built houses away from Leif's, and it is known

from other sources that people like the aforementioned Bishop Gnuppsson went searching for Vinland for some time afterwards. Lee believes that the Pamiok houses' architectural style is as late as that of the 1100s, but from the scarcity of deposits in the associated refuse pile he concludes that occupation of the houses was not of long duration.[32] This is perfectly consistent with Bishop Gnuppsson's voyage of around 1117–21. The Canadian writer Farley Mowat has seen these ruins as well as many of the others in Ungava and commented, "I think we have to believe that navigation in Ungava Bay was almost routine for the Norse, and was carried on for a very long time. Maybe a century."[33] This estimate almost perfectly covers the time period from Leif Eiriksson to Bishop Gnuppsson, after which there is no further record of voyages to Vinland.

If these Pamiok houses are at all connected with Vinland-faring, which now seems highly likely, then they surely, somewhere, contain priceless clues to the actual location of Leif's own house. Meanwhile, these ruins, and especially all the other Norse ruins in Ungava, certainly deserve physical and governmental protection at least equal to that which those in Newfoundland receive.[34]

I conclude that these ruins do constitute corroboration of my theory that Vinland was the west shore of Ungava Bay. And I believe that when the true site of Leif's own house is finally proved, it will prove to be one of those very sites that, as previously mentioned, are currently being discovered in Ungava almost annually. They must be protected, for they contain memorials of world-wide significance.

CHAPTER 5

Traces on the Maps of History

Most modern scholars now accept that in sailing to Vinland the Norsemen had indeed discovered America. But these scholars deprive that conclusion of much of the interest it might otherwise have by pointing out three "facts." First, that there is no evidence that after their first vain attempts the Norsemen ever returned again to Vinland to found permanent settlements. Second, that the Vinland sagas were valued by the Norsemen strictly as family history, and that their geographical aspects held no particular interest for anybody until post-Columbian times. Third, that these sagas were unknown in southern Europe and could not have provided any stimulus to explorers such as Columbus. Thus, as far as any historic heritage is concerned, these scholars say, the Norse discovery in Vinland was no more important than if Vinland had been an insignificant rocky shoal anywhere in the middle of the ocean. Since most scholars deny that the sagas of the discovery of America in Vinland could have influenced the European "Age of Discovery," some other medium of communication must be posited as the basis for my contention that explorations by Leif's successors defi-

nitely sparked Columbus. There are many other sources besides the sagas which shed light on the Norse activities beyond Greenland. There are archaeological findings, Eskimo
folk tales, the *Annals of Iceland* and a host of isolated documents.

Among the most exciting forms of documentary sources,
when they become available, are old maps that have been
overlooked. The extent to which this is true is proved by the
enthusiasm with which the world greeted the discovery of
the Yale Vinland Map in 1965. Unfortunately, as some
scholars subsequently concluded, this particular map provided no new information on the Norse activities.[1] It is my
contention, however, that both the Yale Vinland Map *and a
very large number of other pre-Columbian maps of the Old
World* do show previously unrecognized parts of North
America. Many of these maps have lain under the noses of
historians for centuries, but have escaped notice because
their information is in seemingly incomprehensible, distorted form.

Analysis of these distortions requires painstaking examina-
tions, which I have carried out in a separate study. The distortions are all systematic, and once perceived they leave
little room for doubt about what lands the maps depict. Indeed, the nature of the systematic distortion is often simply
that the American lands have been misplaced into the Old
World map of Eurasia. Suffice it to say, these maps thoroughly undermine the widespread assumption that all
Norse exploration took place solely along the presently inhabited eastern seaboard of America. The maps, surpris-
ingly, show lands of the arctic and sub-arctic regions of
North America, of territory stretching, on the endpaper map,
from Greenland to Alaska. They include detailed maps of
Greenland's immediate western neighbor, Baffin Island, the

Arctic Archipelago north of Canada and the Canadian arctic coast. While publication economics dictate that the many dozens of documentations of this claim be left for a separate study, the illustration of the concept on page 89 may meanwhile somewhat relieve the strain of accepting it on faith.

That the Norsemen could have possessed such an intimate knowledge of the Arctic Archipelago or even Baffin Island seems very surprising. Even more surprising seems the suggestion that they preserved the knowledge in cartographic form. The Norse sailors themselves have never been known to have made or used sailing charts or maps, and the earliest known native Icelandic map was not made until a century *after* Columbus in 1590. Scandinavia itself was not seriously mapped by its native geographers until 1532. Indeed, the native cartographical knowledge of Scandinavia was so inadequate that as late as 1070 the historian Adam of Bremen could not say definitely whether Scandinavia was an island or had a connection to the mainland.[2]

Modern scholars, for apparently good reasons, are so set against the idea that the medieval Norsemen could have made maps that it is necessary to give a full analysis of an alternate means of "explaining away" the maps referred to. The alternate explanation seems simple and straightforward, but, as I will ultimately show, deceptively so. Namely, from the time of the aforementioned Karlsefni's voyage to Vinland the Norsemen had contact with a people who are *known* to have been good geographers and map makers, the Thule Culture Eskimos of North America.

Karlsefni met a race of people in Vinland whom he and the Greenlanders called "Skraellings." These are generally believed to have been Eskimos, although some writers believe they were Indians. I am no better qualified in ethnol-

ogy than most other writers who have speculated on this
question, and I will refrain from joining the controversy and
merely state my belief. The main reason for interest in the
question relates to its geographical implications for the location of Vinland, and that geographical question has been
handled separately here. Plainly and simply, I believe that
the "Skraelings" were in fact Thule Eskimos, newly arrived
to Vinland.

The four centuries of possible contact between the
Norsemen and the Eskimos neatly bracket the recognized
terminal phase of a major eastward migration of the Thule
Eskimos which ended in Greenland.* By the time the Norsemen discovered Vinland around 1000 the Thule Eskimos
had entered Baffin Island from the western neighboring islands of the Arctic Archipelago. During subsequent centuries they crossed Ellesmere Island, entered northern
Greenland and, heading southward, by the late 1200s began
having contact with the Norse settlers from southern Greenland. The contacts were bound to be friendly enough, considering the generally amicable nature of the Eskimo,[4] but
ecclesiastical law limited the Norsemen's contact with the
"heathens" until the next century, when greater fraterniza-
tion became accepted.

The migration of the Thule Eskimos can be traced from
across northern Canada as far as the Coppermine River at
the west end of Coronation Gulf,[5] and ultimately from
their original home in Alaska.[6] Thus, the wandering Eskimos with whom the Norsemen had contact had started in

* It must be emphasized that we are talking about a specific culture
group of Eskimos, the Thule Culture. Previous cultures of Eskimos
lived in Greenland long before the Norsemen arrived, and the Norsemen found remnant traces of their earlier habitations.[3] Other culture
groups, particularly the Dorsets, will be discussed below.

Alaska and were just finishing their migration across the entire North American continent.

These Eskimos were expert map makers, to the point of using crosshatching to depict terrain relief and showing sailing directions between islands.[7] Unfortunately, they had little means of making hard-copy maps, and usually traced them out in the sand or snow from memory when travelers required guidance from them. When modern ninteenth- and twentieth-century explorers presented them with paper and pencil, the Eskimos were overjoyed at being able to make permanent hard-copy maps without the bother of wood carving, and eagerly displayed their cartographic knowledge of far-distant places.[8]

In view of these facts, a more conservative alternative seems available for explaining the existence of the already mentioned pre-Columbian maps of North American arctic lands than the attribution of them to Norse explorations. While the conservative hypothesis will later have to yield in many respects to the radical one, it is, nevertheless, proper to start the analysis with the more conservative hypothesis: that geographical information on the Thule Eskimo migration, including allegedly Eskimo-drawn maps brought from as far away as Alaska, was received in Europe and *incorporated into maps* of the otherwise unknown north of *the Old World.*

Analysis of this hypothesis brings one immediately into confrontation with the question of the contact between the Norsemen and the Eskimos, which is as poorly documented as the rest of the Norse activities. But we know that such contact began when Karlsefni's expedition undertook trade with the Vinland natives around 1010 and, for our present purposes, ended when the Greenland settlements mysteriously disappeared after 1410. During those four centuries there existed an avenue of travel whereby Eskimo maps could find their way to the boards of southern European cartographers, and there for a large variety of good reasons could be totally misunderstood.

The basis of communication between the Eskimos and Norsemen is analyzed in Chapter 7, but it can easily be seen even in the absence of detailed documentation of its nature. The extension of this communication line from the Norsemen to scholars in the south of Europe and its likelihood of generating misunderstanding is what must be closely examined here.

First, Scandinavia seemed psychologically even more remote than the Orient to medieval scholars. This was largely because of the comparison frequently drawn between the high oriental culture and that of the "barbaric" Norsemen. The northern fringe of Scandinavia was mapped just as unknowledgeably as the Orient, in spite of its actual relative proximity, and thus any cartographic information whatsoever coming via the northern sources would have been eagerly consumed. Indeed, the acknowledged sparseness of documentary records of the ancient Norse activities should not suggest that the Norsemen were completely isolated from communication with the south. On the contrary, nearly every existing piece of documentation, including the Norse sagas, indicates communication with the south—but communication took place via laymen who were not particularly interested in cartography.

Second, the avenue for potential misunderstanding was in fact probably broadened by a later European desertion of the Greenland settlers—the general European political unrest which helped bring about the desertion also opened the way for a multitude of pirates and privateers who roamed the seas in search of unprotected settlements such as Greenland, preyed upon one another and sought such distant places of hiding.[9] The three-way contact between this pirate element, the remains of Norse culture in Greenland and European collectors of seafarers' stories could have led only to a distorted information transfer at best, but, as the many Old World maps depicting American lands demonstrate, an active one.

The natures of the misunderstandings along this line of communication are subject to analysis. First, there exists a large number of maps showing evidence for what I shall call the Grand Misunderstanding. By this I mean a misconception that the unrecognized North American continent was actually the known Eurasian continent seen from the opposite end. In maps displaying the Grand Misunderstanding, the pictures of the American lands were attached to the Old World map at their actual relative positions on the North American continent. Thus, for example, Alaska would take the place of northernmost Scandinavia's Lapland.

How could such a misunderstanding be possible? The answer comes from several quarters. There was, it must be remembered, no conception of the Western Hemisphere in pre-Columbian times, and the idea was universally accepted that there was a single inhabited world continent, Africa-Eurasia. The precise meaning of the Latin word *terra*, when used in a geographic sense, was "the world continent."[10] This would have guaranteed the placement of any Eskimo map of Alaska in Lapland, for Eskimo information would have described the homeland in Alaska as being at the northwest corner of *the* continent, and this could only have been identified in Europe with northern Scandinavia. Thus, by mistakenly identifying the Eskimos as a people from northern Scandinavia, the vacuum of Norse cartography would have been filled. Even the Scandinavians themselves, indeed perhaps most of all, would have been prepared to accept the identification of the Eskimos with the poorly known, at that time almost mythical Lapps of northernmost Scandinavia. Both were of Mongoloid racial appearance, shorter than the European in stature and, compared to the southern Scandinavians, technologically primitive.

The misidentification of the Eskimos as a northern Eurasian people would have been further supported by the complicated history of a popular myth. That was the myth of a people called the "Arimphians" in northern Eurasia and the equally mythical Riphean Mountains. The ancient geographer Herodotus (484–424 B.C.) described a people he called "Argippae" as among the northernmost people known, and they were placed at the foot of the "Riphean Mountains." At that time "northernmost" was not very far north, and the Riphean Mountains probably referred to the Balkans.[11] However, as knowledge of the north of the world increased and new people became known, the names of Riphean and Arimphian were not discarded but rather ascribed to people and places farther northward. The names were always associated with peoples and places on the border of the northern Unknown.

By the time of the geographer Mela (A.D. 43) the Riphean Mountains may already have been identified with the Urals and the Arimphians with the Mongols. The myth then became dormant during the depths of the Dark Ages, but in the thirteenth century the Psalter map again showed the Ripheans at the northern edge of the continent with a nearby people called "Arumpheie." By this time the only factual basis for the validity of such a myth in Asia would have been the existence of the arctic peoples of northern Siberia, with the Riphean Mountains being placed east of the Lena River. However, it is highly unlikely that the Europeans had any knowledge of these people, whereas they did have an avenue of contact with the American Eskimos. The earlier identification of the Arimphians with the Mongols certainly would have set the stage for their later identification with the Eskimos, for the felt-covered circular tents of the Mongols[12] correspond closely to the hide-covered circular summer dwellings of the Thule Eskimos. Evidently the time for the identification of the Arimphians with the Eskimos did arrive prior to 1508, for at that time a map by one Johann Ruysch showed one of his four North Polar Islands labeled as "Aronpheie." That Ruysch definitely referred to American Eskimos is evidenced by his inscription in the Bay of Greenland where he virtually beseeched or commanded the inhabitants, "Become you Arumfia; other times they call you Cibes." This imperative is explained by a general belief held at the time that the by then deserted American Norsemen, evidently known to Ruysch otherwise as "Cibes," were "going Eskimo" and losing their original cultural characteristics—that is, "becoming Arimphians."

A further example of an occurrence of the Grand Misunderstanding, identifying the New World as the Old, occurs in a different context not involving maps, but rather a folk story. Throughout the history of the north there recurs in various forms the story of a man, frequently said to be from northern Scandinavia or Lapland, who makes a long journey to the east or to the west and ends up in his homeland, having circled the northern part of the globe.[13] This basic recurrent story has the ring of some misunderstanding of an attempt by a Thule Eskimo brought to the Norwegian court to explain the migration of his people from Alaska, while the listeners identified Alaska with Lapland. The story has naturally taken on varied forms in the course of its retelling.

Sometimes the journey is on foot, as in the tale of the Greenlander Halli Geit:

He alone succeeded in coming by land on foot over mountains
and glaciers and all the wastes, and past all the gulfs of the sea
to Gandvicus [the White Sea] and then to Norway. He led with
him a goat, and lived on its milk; he often found valleys and
narrow openings between the glaciers, so that the goat could
feed either on grass or in the woods.

One of the more picturesque versions of the story is told
by the traveler John Mandeville shortly before 1371, where
he says that

. . . when he was younger he heard of a man who set out from
England to explore the world who went past India [meaning
China in those days] and the islands beyond it, where there are
more than five thousand islands, and so far did he travel over
sea and land that he finally came to an island where he heard
them calling the ox at the plow in his own language, as they did
in his own country. This land afterwards proved to be in Norway.[14]

Thus from the start, from the time this story originated, the
Norwegians would have conceived of a semi-circumnaviga-
tion of the globe, meeting the migrating "pseudo-Lapland-
ers" halfway in Greenland.

The problem of the Middle Ages, it must be stressed, was
not conceiving of the earth as a sphere—the evidence for
sphericity was well known.[15] Rather, the problem of this
peculiar era was to prove, in spite of the evidence, that it
was *not* a sphere.[16] For the logical thinking leading to belief in the world's sphericity was equated with the paganism
of its Roman and Greek originators, while the Bible's Old
Testament necessarily spoke in terms of the flat-disk theory

which existed in pre-Graeco/Roman antiquity. Nevertheless, in spite of the best efforts of many scholarly medieval
monks to impose a literal interpretation of the Old Testament,[17] the awareness of the sphericity of the earth per-
sisted in many European minds.[18] The scholar in his cell
devoutly paid homage to a flat earth while the sailor watching the height of the pole star never doubted sphericity. This
must have been so in the north especially, for there would
have been no other way to explain the behavior of the mid-
night sun so familiar in those latitudes, except by the notion
of the spherical earth.

The Norwegian listeners to the hypothetical Eskimo's
migration story, recounted above in presumably modified
forms, would of course not have suspected the existence of a
"New World." The Eskimos would not have suspected an
"Old World." The misunderstanding of both as the same
would have easily been mutually agreed upon. Helge Ingstad, who lived for a time with the Eskimos, has remarked
upon their innate desire to agree with the white man's
theories.[19] The existence of stories such as this makes it
seem entirely conceivable that map makers, too, would have
been prone to the Grand Misunderstanding.

Detailed study of many maps of the era shows that the
vacuum of Norse cartography undoubtedly was filled by
information from allegedly Eskimo origins. But not only the
Grand Misunderstanding of North America as Eurasia is in
evidence in these maps. Another type of misunderstanding,
which I shall call the Smaller Misunderstanding, was also
present. This had to do not with geographical theory but
with the fact that many of the maps of the American lands
which the southern European scholars attached to their
Old World maps must have come to those scholars without
any understandable explanation of just what lands were

being portrayed on the maps. The maps had reached the scholars from the Norsemen by way of Scandinavia. Thus, the scholars mistakenly concluded that they were maps *of* Scandinavia. They were unaware of previous links in the communications line. In other words, the Smaller Misunderstanding by the southern European cartographers was to equate the unknown *subject* of the strange new maps with the also unfamiliar land of their immediate *provenance*. In contrast to the Grand Misunderstanding—under which logically only the picture of Alaska could appear in the position of Scandinavia—the Smaller Misunderstanding allowed maps of *various* parts of North America, which arrived in Europe via the Scandinavians, to appear on the European map at the position of their *apparent source*—Scandinavia.

Chronological ordering of the maps and stories discloses an orderly evolution of the cartography of Scandinavia when viewed in terms of my hypothesis of these above-described misunderstandings. A synopsis of the events in that chronology follows.

The earliest European maps all depict Scandinavia as an island north of the main continent, separated from it in each case by varying amounts of water and reflecting a total lack of awareness by the cartographers of its ultimate connection to the mainland. The earliest departures from this picture of the land do not seem to be correlated with any known native Scandinavian mapping surveys. Rather, occurrence of a new picture seems to follow quickly after the visit of the aforementioned Icelandic trader, Thorfinn Karlsefni, to the newly discovered Vinland around 1010, where he met the Eskimos who had migrated from Alaska. Karlsefni took several of these Skraelings from Vinland back with him to Iceland, and they told stories of their life which presumably would have been relayed by the world trader

Karlsefni, on other voyages, to European scholars. From this time forward the European maps showed symptoms of the occurrence of the Grand Misunderstanding: They began connecting or replacing the Scandinavian "island" with mainland peninsulas of the Alaskan type, presumably motivated by the Eskimos' migration story.

Subsequent to this incident involving Karlsefni, European contact with the Skraellings was apparently interrupted, and the last record of Norse travel to any country named Vinland was in 1117 when the aforementioned would-be bishop named Eric Gnuppsson attempted to go there. In the absence of further contact with Vinland or, temporarily, the Eskimos, European maps began the tradition of portraying the peninsulas derived from Alaska as an isthmus between the classical Scandinavian island and the mainland.

For 250 years, until the late 1200s, the settlements in Greenland prospered and grew to a population of several thousand. The so-called "Eastern Settlement" was located near the endpaper map's modern Julianehaab, and the "Western Settlement" was actually four hundred miles to the north at Godthaab. The Greenlanders carried out a lively specialty trade with Europe involving native animals such as polar bears and white falcons. Polar bears do not inhabit northern Europe and were highly coveted by rare-animal collectors. Falconry, the "sport of kings," was such a fever that prominent priests occasionally received dispensations to serve mass in hunting gear with falcon perched on the altar waiting for mass to be over,[20] and the Holy Roman Emperor Frederick II spent the latter part of his life writing an encyclopedic masterpiece on the subject. The most prized falcons were the pure white gyrfalcons, which exist only in Greenland and the American arctic.[21] The Greenlanders, then, were known throughout Europe through their trade, in spite of their lack of appearance on any surviving map of the period.

During the thirteenth century the oral sagas were recorded on parchment in Iceland, and in a climate of preoccupation with the "earthly paradise" and the Fortunate Isles, Vinland came to be remembered as "Vinland the Good."

The Greenlanders frequently traveled northward along their island to an area they called *Nordrsetur,* where they found excellent seal and walrus hunting grounds. The limits of this area were undefined, but the stone inscribed with Norse runic characters in Plate 12 has been found far north at the island Kingigtorssuaq, near the area labeled Svartenhuk on the endpaper map. In this area in 1266 the Greenlanders, for the first time since Vinland, re-established contact with the Thule Eskimos, who had meanwhile migrated up through the Arctic Archipelago and then down through Greenland, southward along its west coast.

Immediately following this renewed contact, the European maps of Scandinavia again changed in the continued absence of native Scandinavian mapping surveys. This time the peninsulas of Alaska disappeared from maps of the area and their place was taken by pictures of the islands of the Arctic Archipelago. Evidently Eskimo maps of the places *they* had recently left reached Europe via the Greenlanders and Norway, and it was assumed in Europe that since these maps came through a Scandinavian country they must be maps of Scandinavia—the Smaller Misunderstanding.

Maps involving the Smaller Misunderstanding of a variety of American lands as Scandinavian continued to appear for more than a century. When one examines the detailed chronological sequence in which this phenomenon occurred it seems that the appearance of American lands on the various maps was not without some order. The earliest maps show first perhaps Ellesmere Island, the immediate neighbor of northern Greenland, and then Baffin Island, farther south. Only later do maps of the islands of the central Arctic, on the endpaper map, seem to appear. It becomes evident that in the sequence of these maps a sequence of adjacent geographical locations is being spelled out step by step, defining a route from northern Greenland southward through the archipelago and then westward. It happens that this sequence of geographical locations is the exact *reverse* of the known path of migration of the Thule Eskimos from western Canada eastward into Greenland. Could this be evidence of some of the Eskimos turning around and returning to their original home, or evidence of the Norsemen trying to find where the Eskimos came from? Some light may be shed on this question by the remaining events in this synopsis of the Greenlanders' chronology.

While this curious cartographic evolution was occurring in Europe, a major social evolution was taking place in the Greenland settlements, especially in the Western, as a result of the new contact with the Eskimos. The Greenlanders, by now thoroughly Christianized, were forbidden by the Church to have any contact with the pagans, but as the Thule migration continued southward in Greenland, contact was inevitable. The result was not strife with the Eskimos but, rather, change in the local Church's attitude. Indeed, contact with the Eskimos became accepted to such an extent that the Greenlanders were accused (wrongly) by European churchmen of apostasy and heathenism.

One such churchman named Ivar Bardsson was sent from the archdiocese in Norway to live in Greenland and investigate the situation. His report suggests that the members of the relatively isolated Western Settlement had established such friendly contacts with the Eskimos that they were vacating their agricultural settlement and dispersing into Eskimo hunting lands. Bardsson saw to it that this resulted in ostracism by and from the Eastern Settlement, which had closer ties to Europe and the Church. Bardsson's successors in the Eastern Settlement, however, showed increasing tolerance to Eskimo contact until, near the end of the fourteenth century, a traveler named Zeno described the situation at a Norse monastery that some writers interpret to be located in the Eastern Settlement. If Zeno's controversial report is to be believed, it shows that even the monks had turned to use of the Eskimo kayak and Eskimo housebuilding methods, that agriculture was replaced by hunting (except for a trick vegetable garden in the hot springs), and that woven cloth was considered a luxury import. Nevertheless, the members of the Eastern Settlement were still Christians.

Concluding the synopsis of the chronology we have been tracing, a final glimpse of the Greenland settlement is given in a letter from Pope Nicholas V in which he describes a series of pirate attacks in 1418 on the Eastern Settlement, during which many of the inhabitants were carried away into slavery and the buildings burned. The classical theory on the fate of the Greenland settlements is that this pirate destruction marked the end of the Norse people in the Western Hemisphere. But it remains to be seen whether this classical idea can continue to stand in the face of subsequent developments.

Plainly and simply, it was only after this supposed extinction that the most detailed and most unmistakable maps of North American lands began to appear on European maps. Where could they have come from if the Greenlanders were no longer there to transmit them? Such maps continued to

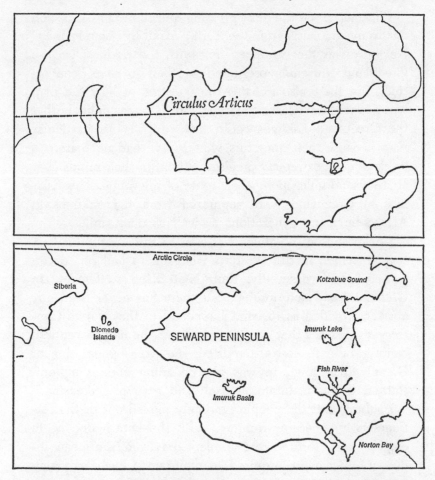

Portion of 1427 map (see Plate 15) "of Scandinavia" by Claudius Clavus (top), compared with Alaska's Seward Peninsula (bottom).

appear throughout the fifteenth century and into the next. One of the most spectacular of these, Plate 15, drawn at Rome in 1427 by one Claudius Clavus, depicted the Bering Strait area of Alaska with Seward Peninsula in precise detail, as shown by the above comparison figure.

This map poses the most pressing question: How did such a map make its way from the Bering Strait to Rome in 1427? Not only was the European link with the Eskimos via the Greenland Norsemen presumed by then to have been extinct, but there also remains the question of how the map was passed from Alaska to Greenland. It seems unlikely that the Greenland Eskimos could have drawn this particular map because their ancestors would have had no reason to transmit such extremely precise material in their minds over six thousand miles along their route of migration. The Eskimos in Greenland were separated from the Eskimos in Alaska by many generations as well as many miles.

I propose that the obvious answer to this question is that the Norsemen in the Western Hemisphere had not disappeared at all. Assuredly, their centralized *settlements* in Greenland had deteriorated, but there has never been any answer provided as to what happened to the *people*. Contrary to theories that were in vogue in the early twentieth century but are now discredited, the Norse population of Greenland as a group was not declining and dying out. Rather, it was maintaining itself and perhaps increasing.[22]

I submit that the people gradually moved out of the settlements and became hunters. With the known decline in contact with Europe, the implements from European industry which were required to maintain a husbandry culture became scarce and the need to supplement farming by hunting increased. An even more important climatic factor in the shift away from farming, the "Little Ice Age," is discussed in Chapter 8. A direct result of even the slightest shift away from a husbandry culture would have been the further breaking of ties with the Norsemen by Europe, thereby increasing even more the Norse dependence on hunting. This is an unending circle. But probably the strongest influence on this process of isolating the Norse, from the European point of view, was the rumor that the Greenlanders, because of their contacts with the Eskimo culture, were turning away from Christianity.

A most important direct result of the shift towards hunting would have been a strong need for dispersal of the population. This has nothing to do with overpopulation or any instinctive drive for emigration. It is simply the nature of hunting that any culture which depends upon hunting must necessarily be dispersed. Wild animals soon enough learn to avoid any permanent settlement. Thus, anybody who looks for the last American Norsemen in the Greenland ruins is bound to be disappointed.

Indeed, it is worthwhile to recall that from shortly after the re-established contact with the Eskimos in 1266, there exists a definite chronological-geographical sequence of maps extending *backwards* along the route of the Thule migration. Instead of attributing these maps to Eskimos, might it not also be reasonable—indeed perhaps more reasonable—to view them as a history of Norse *forward* dispersal into lands the Thules told them about? With their ships, the Norsemen could in one or two summers make the voyage between Alaska and Greenland which had taken the Eskimo people centuries to accomplish. (It is not really necessary to have steel-bowed supertankers with gigantic engines to sail through the Northwest Passage so long as one does have patience, understanding of ice conditions and skill in ship handling.[23] Whalers sailed their wooden ships through the Arctic's ice[24] for several centuries before Amundsen negotiated the Passage—in a ship smaller than many Norse ships.) The 1427 map of Clavus would be the natural end result of a westward dispersal. Surely the Greenland Norsemen must have learned the technical concepts of

map making from the Thule Eskimos shortly after their first
contacts in the thirteenth century. And, they also had access
to writing materials from that time, when the sagas were
first written down, onward. This hypothesis of a westward
Norse dispersal is examined in Chapter 8 in much greater
detail for, even though it may have been made to seem
plausible, it has admittedly not been proven by any of the
foregoing.

The first problem that demands attention, concerns how
it was that these maps could have reached Europe after the
European trade with Greenland ceased. It is of course possible to speculate that if the Norsemen remaining in America
were capable of sailing between Alaska and Greenland, they
could also sail back across the Atlantic. However, one would
have to ask why they should be motivated to do so since
their culture had by now presumably broken with Europe,
and vice versa. Furthermore, a ship capable of sailing about
the waters of the Arctic is not necessarily capable of sailing
across the Atlantic. Even if they had had a proper ship, it
is questionable if these American Norsemen would have
even known how to sail back to Europe any more for the
Greenland trade had been made a Norwegian royal monopoly in 1294, and since then the only ships allowed to make
the trip had been the royal merchant ships whose crews
were Norwegian. In any case, if such travelers had by some
means made their way to Norway they would have attracted
so much attention that it would seem fair to assume that
the event would have been clearly recorded, and no such
record exists.

However, there exists another form of historical record
that may give a hint at an alternative means of transmission
of the maps across the Atlantic—on the ships of *pirates*.
The introduction of the evidence for pirate transmission re-

quires some digression. When Greenland was "rediscovered" in the modern era, the Scandinavian countries naturally took a great interest in the possibility of finding descendants of the earlier settlers, but they were prepared for the possibility that the old Norse culture had been absorbed into the heathen Eskimo culture. The first man to conduct thorough exploration for these people was the Danish missionary Hans Egede in 1721, who intended to either convert the surviving Norsemen from presumed heathenism back to Christianity or, if they were still Christian, from Catholicism to Lutherism. Egede spent many years in Greenland and discovered the ruins of the ancient Norse settlements, but found no people except Eskimos. However, his son Niels, who grew up in Greenland and spoke Eskimo like a native, collected several Eskimo folk tales that are very much part of the historical record that serious scholars must take into consideration. One narrative that Helge Ingstad has translated from Niels' diary suggests a continuing trans-Atlantic contact with Greenland after the pirate destruction of 1418 reported in the letter of Pope Nicholas V, described above. The story was told to Egede by an eighteenth-century Eskimo from the neighborhood of the old Eastern Settlement.

He told me that his forefathers had related that when their forefathers came from North America [via the archipelago] and advanced southward upon the western side of Greenland to settle, some desired to live among the Norwegians [Norse Greenlanders], who forbade them, and would permit them only to trade with them. We [Eskimos] were afraid of them, since they had many kinds of firearms.* But when a number of families had

* Knowledge of the early history of firearms is vague, but it is highly unlikely that the Norsemen had any firearms when the first Eskimos arrived. Most likely this is a substitution of a modern word for an older Eskimo phrase relating to the Norsemen's steel swords and axes, more frightening to the primitive Eskimos than unfamiliar guns.

gathered and come upon a more cordial footing with them, there came from the Southwest three small ships, and plundered and killed some of the Norwegians; yet as the Norwegians over-mastered them, the second ship sailed away and the third they took as prize, but we [Eskimos] having no fixed dwelling at that time, were afraid and fled far into the country. But the following year there came a whole fleet and fought with them, plunder-ing and slaying wantonly, carrying off their cattle and furniture and then sailed away. Those who remained shoved out their open boats and went aboard, and sailed to the southerly part of the country, leaving some behind. Our [Eskimos] promised to stand by them in support if more such evils should occur.

But the following year those wicked pirates came again and when we saw them we fled and took some of the Norwegian women and children with us up the fiord, leaving the others in the lurch; but when in the autumn we returned, thinking to find some of them, we saw with horror that everything had been carried off, houses and farms burnt and laid waste so that everything was lacking. At this sight we took the women and children back with us and fled far up the fiord, and there we re-mained at peace for many years. We married the Norwegian women, five in number, with some children. When in time we became numerous we travelled about and settled down along the land, and for many years saw no more of the pirates. At last one came, which was one of the English privateers, and when they saw that we possessed but little and that we were many they did not venture to come against us, but traded only. This same kind of people still come here from time to time to trade with the [Eskimos] and when they find an opportunity to do it they rob everywhere, so it is likely that these sea-rovers were the same; and they now have colonies over against us in the American settlements.[25]

The continuing contact of the privateers is a possible an-swer to the question of how maps of American lands kept reaching Europe after recognized contact with Greenland ceased. While our impression of their activities is not always

as being very glamorous, many privateers were in fact
warmly received in European social and scholarly circles.
As Ingstad points out,[26] this narrative bears all the marks of
authenticity and shows no tendency toward the distortions
found in some Eskimo folk tales. One need not be particularly disturbed by the fact that it was told and recorded
almost three centuries following the events described. This
situation is comparable to that of the period between the
secretive 1576–78 gold-hunting voyages of Martin Frobisher
and the actual discovery of Frobisher's barren mining sites
by Hall in 1860, based on Eskimo narratives.[27] The Homeric
legends of Greece were simply that—legends—until Heinrich
Schliemann's excavations gave them substance. From this
fact it became apparent that it was possible for oral tradition to preserve facts accurately through the centuries. It
would be tempting to speculate about the Eskimos acquiring
a saga-telling tradition from the Norsemen, permitting the
story to be told unaltered from its original form and re-
taining the identification of the pirates as English, certainly
a meaningless identification to the intervening generations
of Eskimos.

In fact, the year of the pirate sack of Greenland was just
at the beginning of the era (1420s) when many pirates
known to be English were making repeated attacks on Iceland and carrying away into slavery all the people they
could. It would have been natural for them to start their
human hunting in the least protected areas such as Greenland, and just as natural for them to lay waste to the buildings that would have been potential defense fortresses in
later attacks. The Eskimo narrative suggests that there was
a pirate lair southwest of Greenland, perhaps on the American continent. That the English did make subsequent visits,
although more peaceful, is attested not only by the Eskimo

narrative but also by circumstantial evidence which demonstrates that the English later actually returned many of the kidnapped Greenlanders. Such evidence is contained in the letter of Pope Nicholas V, which after describing the attacks says, ". . . the greater number have since returned from this captivity to their own homes and have here and there repaired the ruins of their dwellings . . ." This return presumably was necessitated by the treaty of 1432 between the English and Norwegian kings, which specified not only the return of prisoners from such raids to their homelands, but punishment for English subjects who engaged in any further such practices.

The enforcement of such requirements is not a matter of record, but it is clear that the English pirates and privateers now at least had the sailing directions to Greenland. In fact, they probably had had them since the writing of a book called the *Inventio Fortunatae* in 1363 by an English author describing his trip throughout the north. It is known that after the *Inventio* was published its author returned to those northern environs five different times on "King's business," and thus most likely on English ships, whose crews would have learned the sailing directions.

Herein, in the dissemination of the sailing directions to Greenland among the pirates, if not even among regular English sailors, lies a basis for a plausible continuation of contact between Europe and the Norsemen in America. Pirates, privateers and sailors on their own accounts did not discontinue their activities but rather increased them greatly[28] during the fifteenth and sixteenth centuries.

The main slave market of the north was in Bristol, and it was the Bristol merchants who sponsored the highly questionable "explorations" of John Cabot, first official discoverer of the same general area from which the 1418 pirates based their attack on Greenland. From Bristol alone, there are more than twenty licenses or proceedings still known from the fifteenth century concerning illegal private trade with Iceland.[29] While we have no proof and, because of the clandestine nature of the activities, probably never will, it is not difficult to imagine a continuing link with Greenland via Bristol. Such a link would have continued even after Europe's communication with Greenland via Norway was terminated by Norway's preoccupation with the Hanseatic League and European politics. In any case, we can be certain that there was some kind of contact between Greenland and Europe subsequent to the "classical" period ending in 1400, because graves have been found in Greenland containing European fashions from the *late* 1400s.[30]

The area southwest of Greenland, from which the pirates in the Eskimo narrative are supposed to have sprung their attacks, is represented on many pre-Columbian maps. Perhaps the most important of these are a group from the fifteenth century and later which all seem to show the sub-continental, wedge-shaped Quebec/Labrador Peninsula, on the endpaper map, bounded on the west by Hudson Bay and James Bay, the northeast by the Labrador Sea, and the southeast by the St. Lawrence estuary.

Thule Eskimos are never known to have migrated so far south, and those maps cannot lightly be attributed to them. Furthermore, some of those maps show effects of magnetic compass variation. The Eskimos did not use compasses, but the later medieval Norsemen did. If it can be concluded that Norsemen explored this part of America in the fifteenth century, and Chapter 9 shows that it can, then these explorations were even more important than the Vinland explorations. For, while the Vinland explorations were ultimately forgotten, those of the fifteenth century, although misunderstood, were recorded and discussed by southern European scholars, just before the so-called Age of Discovery.

CHAPTER 6

The Columbus Controversy

In spite of everything that has been said so far in this volume, there will still be those who will always want to insist that, no matter what the Norsemen did, Columbus was still the proper, honest-to-goodness, true discoverer of America. History in the era of the sagas used to consist of the study of isolated heroes and their deeds, but during the Renaissance this interest was gradually expanded to include nations and, eventually, races. In quite recent times the focus of historiography is coming more and more to concentrate on the history of ideas and knowledge rather than just on events and people.[1] Nevertheless, whenever the subject of the discovery of America comes up, one sees an immediate reversion to hero worship. The all-important question becomes, "Was it Christopher Columbus or Leif Eiriksson?" and the implication is that neither camp is willing to concede any significance to the efforts of the other's hero. Colorful writers ranging from Eben Horsford to Michael Musmanno have taken firm and sometimes agitated stands on the subject. Even responsible historians have indignantly dismissed Nordic scholars as creating a myth while they themselves

are promoting a cult of Columbus. One such, Samuel E.
Morison, uses the biblical capitalization to refer to Columbus
as "the Discoverer."[2] While such romanticism is nothing but
amusing to the detached observer, it is, nevertheless, a decided stumbling block to a valid appreciation of history—
particularly the history of ideas.

Future historians will doubtlessly give due credit to the
Americans Armstrong and Aldrin for being the first men on
the moon, and then they will stress these men's dependence
upon men like Stapp and Von Braun. These men, in turn,
were just as dependent upon Newton, who was just as dependent upon Euclid, etc., on into prehistory. But upon
closer examination a question arises as to whether too much
emphasis is not being put on the men themselves rather than
on the processes by which the ideas they are known for
came to a focus in those particular individuals. Indeed, the
conclusion which becomes more and more inescapable, as
the history of ideas is pursued, is that things would be pretty
much the same today if none of these particular men had
ever lived. Each one's discoveries were "in the air" and imminent at the time he lived, and if he himself had not made
them, somebody else would have, albeit perhaps a few years
later.[3] Contemporary researchers who nervously rush to pub-
lish their new results are well aware of this fact of progress.

Thus, in order to gain a true understanding of the Columbian discovery of America, one must look at all the ideas
that were in the air just previous to its occurrence. This
process has, in fact, been under way for the last century at
a rather leisurely pace, and hopefully this study has added
a few significant comments to that survey of ideas. One
realizes that this gigantic task has just begun, however,
when he realizes how many ancient manuscripts there are
still to be read and how often each must be read before

understanding how various ideas are interrelated. Since each reader has a unique point of view on each new manuscript uncovered, the likelihood of historians coming to an immediate consensus is remote indeed.

Nevertheless, regardless of their individual attitudes toward historical determinism, all writers on the subject of Columbus have been curious and dissatisfied about the explanation of Columbus' motivation for his voyage. If his belief that he could reach Asia by sailing westward was based on nothing more than the generally accepted knowledge that the earth was round, it could not possibly have received the interest and backing it did. The romantic idea that few people before Columbus believed in a round earth is just as silly as the idea that nobody thought about gravity until Newton was hit by a falling apple. But the scholars of Columbus' time were quite right in opposing his scheme to sail westward to Asia, because they knew the size of the globe and the safe maximum time at sea for a fully provisioned ship. There was absolutely no hope of Columbus' sailing even one third of the actual distance westward to Asia. But he had somehow convinced himself that the distance was much less and was eventually able to convince his royal backers that the voyage was feasible. In modern terms, the financing for the first voyage came to more than the current buying power of a quarter million dollars,[4] and besides this Columbus was able to bargain in advance for an admiralty, a viceroyship and 10 per cent of all profits. In the absence of *sure* knowledge of *something* out there, Columbus' project appears to be either that of a god or of a naïve self-deceiver who was saved by good luck.

Those writers who have tried to understand Columbus in more human terms have generally come to the conclusion that he had shadowy information, of which we are no longer aware, based on the actual existence of the American continents, but misconstrued as the east coast of Asia. Now while it is clear that widespread knowledge of the Norse activities was available, not only in Iceland but throughout Europe,[5] and that someone other than Columbus soon would have followed it, it is *nevertheless* impossible for me to show any direct *non-circumstantial* evidence that Columbus himself had any of that knowledge.[6] Countless scholars across the centuries have searched his personal records held by his descendants, and if such direct evidence ever existed, it quickly disappeared. Those who choose to are therefore still free to imagine Columbus setting out blindly on a voyage which, without the intervention of Providence and a new continent, would have led him, his associates and their loyal crews to certain death and their King and Queen to ridicule. The rest of us must bide our time until the next discovery in a random unknown library of some dusty manuscript unread in recent centuries, or until some newborn insight into existing records appears. When that time comes, the glory of Columbus will not be diminished but rather increased, for then he will become part of the orderly progress of mankind.

Meanwhile, it is worth examining some of the circumstantial evidence suggesting that Columbus was fired by more than a personal demon. The old idea that he was fired by the writings of the ancients, who said it was theoretically possible to pass westward from Spain to Asia, fails to take into account a certain aspect of human nature. That is, people do not go out of their way to invent rationalizations about scientific measurements, such as the size of the earth, merely for the purpose of proving that the ancients were right. Rather, one might more likely tend to resurrect the writings of the ancients in an attempt to understand some current phenomenon which is perceived but otherwise unexplained. Detailed analysis of pre-Columbian maps, as well as other geographical ideas that were in the air just before the Columbian discovery of America, suggests strongly that such shadowy, frequently misunderstood information did exist, and was based on the dispersal of the Norse settlements in Greenland into America. The misunderstanding that this continental American land was the eastern part of Asia would have been a logical corollary of the same Grand Misunderstanding which placed Alaska in Scandinavia.

This step of misunderstanding was indeed taken by some European scholars just in time for Columbus' rationalizations, but most of the scholars of the time seem only to have arrived with great reluctance at the conclusion that Asia was within reasonable sailing distance westward from Europe. Why? First, I have stated the widespread attitude that all new Scandinavian geographical discoveries to the northwest of Europe must presumably lie in Scandinavia itself. I have referred to this in Chapter 5 as the Smaller Misunderstanding. This attitude, then, would have precluded the Grand Misunderstanding and would have prevented common acceptance of the identification of lands west of Greenland as Asia. A further complication must have been the very fact that while the Eskimo map sources could speak with authority, the "amateur" Norse sources could not, and only with Claudius Clavus in 1427 was the placement of Greenland coming to be taken into account at all in the southern European theoretical picture of the world. Another reason for scholarly reluctance to join in the Grand Misunderstanding may be that as long as the placement of Greenland was explained away hazily, a certain fundamental problem could be avoided. That problem was that once a geographer accepted that Greenland lay just off the coast of Asia he was immediately confronted with a quantitative contradiction. Namely, the sailing distance from Scandinavia westward to Greenland was known and the theoretical distance from Scandinavia eastward to China was known or surmised. And these distances just could not tally up to the size of the earth, correctly known since classical Greek times to be some 24,000 miles. To accept the suggestion of the folk tale in Chapter 5—that people from Norway and Lapland could communicate with one another by traveling in opposite directions around the globe and meeting in Greenland—would have been to overthrow all the scientific measurements of the size of a degree and the circumference of the Earth. But this was precisely the kind of overthrow which did take place by the late 1400s.

Claudius Clavus probably did more than any other geographer to keep the placement of Greenland in doubt, neither associated with the west nor the east, and thus avoided the confrontation of the circumference contradiction. Nevertheless, the very vigor with which he apparently undertook this task suggests that the problem was already making itself strongly felt in the early 1400s. Cassidy[7] believes that some scholars may have associated the Norse discoveries theoretically with Asia as early as 1250. I believe that a Catalan map of 1380 had already broken with the tradition of associating Norse discoveries with the open northwest Atlantic and had associated them with Marco Polo's stories from eastern Asia. Indeed, the Dutchman Jacob Cnoyen had used Polo's names, such as the Province of Bergi, in describing the northwestern explorations in the 1360s.

The reason for the ultimate transition to acceptance of the Grand Misunderstanding of "Greenland in Asia" was presumably that as the Greenlanders spread out over North

America, the reports of the extent of their explorations under their presumed new hunting culture made the lands impossible to rationalize any longer as part of the Scandinavian corner of the world. The only theoretical conclusion available to geographers was that the voyages had gone so far west as to reach eastern Asia. Therewith, throughout the fifteenth century new information began to be displayed in the northeast corner of maps of Asia.

Nowhere in southern Europe, however, was there any *explicit* discussion of the problem of identifying this land to the west. The source of the problem was so far removed from awareness in southern Europe that the geographical community apparently did not realize that it was tackling the problem. (It is now commonly accepted that such an unconscious grappling with problems is an essential part of "progress."[8]) The geographers seem to have made various almost subliminal attempts at dealing with this problem. Dominicus Ducier in 1422 and the anonymous Vienna Klosterneuberg Schyfkart of the middle 1400s showed new land in the west as halfheartedly connected to Europe. Strange projections and cartographic artifices appeared in the disk maps, but none of these were discussed in print. European scholars suddenly took an intense interest in the classical Greek geographer Ptolemy and his theories in the 1400s, to which they could have had access all along. (Was this interest merely an incidental step in the development of Humanism, or was it motivated by an unconscious desire to deal more effectively with rumors of land in the west?)

Regardless of Clavus' obfuscation of Greenland's placement, academic interest in a westward view of eastern Asia increased markedly among the remaining adherents of the medieval wheel-map tradition. This academic interest was growing just at a time when the scholars were being converted to a Ptolemaic theory that forced them to think quantitatively in terms of the entire globe. The result, aided and abetted by Ptolemy's own incorrectly small estimate of the size of a degree[9] and by a longing for Marco Polo's spice islands, was an increasing pressure for downward revision of the concepts of the size of the Earth. It was this revision, necessarily incorrect, that was responsible for getting America "officially" discovered.

Within a short time, people like Doctors Paolo Toscanelli and Hieronoymus Muntzer began discussing the practical possibility of making an actual voyage westward to Asia. From the number of different official proposals to kings on record, it is not difficult to imagine how many less official schemes went unrecorded. Neither is it difficult to imagine that many unrecorded attempts were made before certain people like one John Thloyde and some Bristol voyagers who preceded John Cabot began having recordable success.

The first downward rationalizations of the size of the degree sufficient to force the east coast of Asia to coincide with the east coast of America, as far as is known, seem to have been arrived at by Columbus.[10] However, it would be doing him a dishonor to suggest that such a fantastic rationalization was not already in the air. It would seem that only definite knowledge of land that could not otherwise be accounted for would have called for such mental gymnastics. These rationalizations were eventually able to overcome the objections of royal advisers, and soon thereafter the necessary funding for what was to be the official discovery of America became available.

Donworth finds evidence of foreknowledge in the fact that the distance Columbus expected to sail was exactly the true distance across the North Atlantic.[11] He believes that Columbus learned whatever information he had while he

was visiting Iceland in 1477 and kept this ingredient secret
while working out other aspects of the project.[12] No less a
scholar than Stefansson has suggested that the Spanish
government and the new pope of 1492, a Spaniard, con-
spired to obfuscate previous knowledge of western lands in
favor of Spanish title to the lands.[13] This particular pope,
Alexander VI Borgia, was known as one of the most worldly
popes in history. The Soviet historian and philologist David
Tsukernik finds many indications in the writings of Columbus' crew and associates that the chart by which Columbus
sailed was not just theoretically conceived, but contained
navigational data obtainable only by previous experience in
the area.[14] The British historian David Quinn sees a letter
from John Day giving requested information to Columbus
as evidence that Columbus was motivated by knowledge of
the Bristol activities,[15] which, in turn, I believe to have
been based on Norse knowledge.

Such hypotheses would go far to rescue Columbus from
the picture of an unnecessarily self-deceiving crank setting
out blindly groping on what should have been a 12,000-mile
voyage and being saved at the last moment by the appearance of offshore islands of a previously unknown continent.
Henry Vignaud has constructed an analysis resting on a
belief current in Columbus' time that he had been told of
land in the west by a certain pilot who had been lost, drifted
there and returned. Vignaud's analysis suffers, among other
things, from his unsubstantiated denial of known correspondence between the aforementioned Toscanelli and Columbus, but the story of the pilot remains. The Toscanelli
letter and map themselves have been called upon by some
to explain Columbus' success, but if that map truly had
such an ingredient, it should have brought success to Portugal itself earlier. While other ingredients such as knowl-

edge of Atlantic winds and currents would have been required,[16] the Portuguese sailors certainly had these.

One writer, Jennings Wise, has created a version of history that attributes knowledge of Norse activities not only to Columbus but to all European history preceding Columbus. His theories place the Norsemen, as an arm of the medieval Church, in close contact with Indians as far south as Mexico, and as an arm of the European economy, extracting gold throughout the region.[17] While Wise is an extremely well-read scholar, his theories seem to be based more on attention to ideology and imaginativeness than on critical analysis of evidence. Nevertheless, it is interesting to note that Columbus' contemporary Las Casas evidently interviewed Indians in Cuba and found that:

The neighboring Indians of that island asserted that there arrived to this island of Hispaniola other bearded white men like us, not many years before us.[18]

He recorded this in connection with the story of the lost pilot who supposedly preceded Columbus, but the beards could just as well have been worn by Norsemen as by Spanish conquistadores. It is, of course, now impossible to say if the "not many years" of the Indians was in the range of decades or centuries, but the Indians in any case meant to indicate that other white men had preceded Columbus to the Caribbean. If these men had somehow also encountered the Aztec/Mayan civilizations in nearby Yucatan, or even heard about them through the Cubans, and returned the information to Europe, then one might be able to explain why Marco Polo's extravagant lands of gold began, as with one Albertin de Virga's 1415 map, to be associated with the west instead of the east. Before 1400 Zeno told a story of gold users south of the Norse countries, which would certainly have encouraged belief in the association as well. These stories provide a refutation to the proclamation by some scholars that Columbus could not have been motivated by the Norsemen, because he sailed so far south. If such information, in whatever form and by whatever means, reached Columbus, then it would be not at all surprising that the course he plotted for the golden land of Cathay led him eventually to the latitudes of the Aztecs. Those who wish to may imagine Dominicus Ducier's 1422 map, which shows continental land in the western ocean, as extending to those latitudes, and a scholar of the stature of Cortesão has taken a nautical chart of 1424, which introduced new islands in the western ocean, to represent these very West Indies. The medieval Norsemen tell us in several texts that they believed Vinland was connected with Africa. They may, in saying this, have been letting us know how far south they had gone. Indeed, if North America was taken to be Asia, then South America fits the geographical situation of Africa very accurately in that it is more southerly than the presumed Asia and is connected to it by a narrow isthmus corresponding to Suez.[19] This analogy would have been the ultimate step of the Grand Misunderstanding, equating the entire New World with the entire Old World.

Can any conclusions be drawn from these circumstances? I think so. There exists a group of historical writers who have been willing to admit that there were some Norse activities in America but deny any historical significance to these activities. Even aside from the question of direct Norse influence on Columbus, it now appears that such a stand will have to be modified. There was an unquestionable *indirect* influence of fundamental proportions on Columbus, through the vague ideas of land in the west which were already in the air. The great accomplishment by Columbus was to make the Grand Misunderstanding become accepted, at least temporarily, throughout the rest of the European scholarly world. The originally pagan Norse vitality was a key factor in the general development of the Renaissance[20]—may even have been at the forefront of the original Indo-European push from the steppes into Europe.[21] In fact, these explorers actually contributed the knowledge of their science to the intellectual substance and very being of the Renaissance. When Columbus sailed out into the ocean blue he was headed for lands already vaguely, if not even well known, to many Europeans. And this part of the *Zeitgeist* that made Columbus' voyage possible was created by the Norsemen. Modern America is indeed a Viking America.

How is it, then, that Columbus has been allowed to be elevated onto such a pillar that in some circles he is almost deified? Perhaps some of this comes from the fact that even in his time people were still looking for the earthly paradise, and the qualities of the new land made it seem, in Europe, a paradise. Another reason may be that the history of historiography, nurtured in the study of the Roman Empire, prompts many historiographers still to display frequently a bias favoring anything descendent of the Roman world while denying, or at least minimizing, the importance of anything Teutonic. A still stronger reason, at least in the early post-Columbian days, was probably political. Whenever one sees history being taught in a way different from what actually seems to have happened, one may, I believe, as a generality, look for political motivation.

As soon as a nation discovers new lands, it has new political problems on its hands as well as new assets. It must establish its rightful claim to those assets in the face of possible competition from other nations. When several nations make similar discoveries and the geographical situation of none of these discoveries is quite clear, the problem can become complex indeed.

The most basic recognized ingredient in the European political formula deciding the right to title was originality and precedence of discovery *over other Christian nations*. The effort of all involved nations to establish such claims is a well-known part of the history of the age of discovery. One might think that, given such a formula, Greenlandic foreknowledge of lands thought to be newly discovered by other nations should have been brought to international awareness. However, since political representation of Greenland no longer existed and Norway's own representation had passed to Denmark, it is unreasonable after all to expect this. In fact, any nation outside of Scandinavia having information about such foreknowledge would have done well not to mention it for fear of jeopardizing its own chances to eventually make claims in the "new" lands. To suggest that actual co-ordinated suppression of knowledge took place would be, however, as foolish as most other suggestions of international conspiracies. Nevertheless, it sometimes happens that individual determinations coincide in such a way as to give misleading impressions of conspiracies, especially if those determinations are made at a common subconscious level.

What renaissance Spanish scholar having any political sense would give a second thought to publishing anything detrimental to his sovereigns' claims? What Italian would have any motivation to lessen the glory of Columbus? What English navigator who may even have been to Greenland and now was claiming Newfoundland for England would step forward to deny the rumors that the Greenlanders had deserted Christianity?

Anyway, it is the *scholars* who should have been expected to come forward with the theory that the new lands in the west were the same ones that had been torturing their predecessors' cosmographic theories for the past century. And they do not, in fact, seem to have made the association. They were too busy mapping the "new" lands to be concerned with their predecessors' theoretical struggles with hazy information on the Norse dispersal.

Today there is nothing political to be gained on either side by pitting Columbus against the Norsemen. It is, in fact, possible to see in many maps continuing traces of Norse knowledge of America in the post-Columbian period of European exploration and land claiming. These traces are not quite so patent as pre-Columbian traces because one now has to discriminate between the two possible sources, either Norse maps or actual new discoveries. Nevertheless, it is possible to consider such a discrimination without jeopardizing one's conception of the justness of current national tenure in the Western Hemisphere. Even if the title of the current tenants were contestable, it could be contested by only one body—the medieval free state of Greenland—and it exists no longer.

Given the political death of medieval Greenland, any world-political basis for a cult of Columbus to counteract Greenlandic claims is no longer present, and has not been for some centuries. Nevertheless, it is precisely within the most recent centuries that the glorification of Columbus has proceeded at its fastest pace. I believe that this can be interpreted as a reaction against the rise, during the same period, of the philosophies of determinism. That is to say, Columbus' project has become appropriated, by those who desire to believe they have a free will, as an ultimate expression of the human spirit. He has become the prime example of what one can do if one simply wills to. Evidently, the medieval urge to self-deception is still with us, for, as it now appears, Columbus' success was very much predetermined.

Perhaps the true glory of Columbus lay in his ability, in spite of the incorrectness of his conscious theories, to accept as truth the rumors he probably heard about other people's contact with mainland in the west. He believed so strongly that land lay just where America was to be found that he was willing to confront the entire intellectual establishment. Perhaps the time has come to recognize Columbus as one of those renaissance pioneers in the acceptance of human experience as the basis for modern scientific theorizing.[22] For him to prove the Earth as round would have been trivial compared to what he actually did prove: that attention to experience can open doors to reality which are locked to a man purely of reason.

CHAPTER 7

Norsemen Among the Eskimos

It seems clear from all the foregoing that, as a people, the Norsemen in America had a much richer history than has hitherto been imagined. It is possible to reconstruct some of that history.

As a technical literary device for gathering together all the archaeological and anthropological evidence for that history, I will pay some attention to a possible valid criticism of the argument so far. The criticism is that so far the argument has been based almost entirely on maps and theoretical geographical considerations. All of the maps considered thus far are based on prototypes now lost, probably forever. The fact that no prototypes bearing the signature "Drawn by Norsemen" can be produced necessarily provides an opportunity for the critical mind to assert that, all along, the prototypes were Eskimo maps which made their way to Europe via the Greenland settlement. It is necessary to give this assertion the fullest possible consideration if a reliable basis for historical interpretation is to be established.

The Greenlanders had, as indicated, an intimate contact with the Eskimos; indeed, in later days probably an interdependent one. In exchange for iron tools from the Norsemen, the Eskimos would have been willing to go to great lengths to supply the wants of the Norsemen, even if those wants included a demand for these maps. The critic may postulate an Eskimo sledge trip to Alaska and back, a physical possibility in a matter of a few years, as a means of transporting maps such as Clavus' prototype to Greenland. To me this seems a rather excessive length to go to; but relayed trading routes could have been set up. The observation in Chapter 5, that the historical sequence in which the maps appeared itself suggests a westward exploration by the Greenlanders, has an alternative. The sequence westward could also represent the steps westward in establishing an Eskimo trade chain. The Norsemen could produce items of trade that would have been highly valuable all along such a chain.

But such a critic hypothesizing a trade chain would then have to face the question of what the Norsemen hypothetically got in return. Of what value to them would a map of a distant unknown land have been? Were they selling them to European explorers, only to have them incorrectly incorporated into European maps to confuse other explorers? Were they precious curios whose exchange value was worth spending days over a hot anvil? It would seem that the only value of a map to a Greenland Norseman would have been as a guide of a place to go to or a record of a place already visited.

This kind of reasoning, however, proves nothing. In order to confidently assert that the maps were associated with Norse explorations, independent archaeological evidence that the Norsemen were in those areas would be most helpful. This cannot be produced as fully as one would like, for the archaeology of the northlands is understandably still in a rudimentary state. Even during the short summer seasons when digging can be attempted, one comes in a few inches to permafrost hard as rock; and jackhammers are hardly the tool to go after delicate specimens. (Nevertheless, the permafrost preserves specimens which would otherwise decay.) Furthermore, those excavations that have been accomplished by patiently melting the permafrost, layer by layer, have concentrated almost exclusively on known Eskimo sites. The fact that these excavations have not yielded evidence of a vast chain of intra-Eskimo trade in Norse goods may be a point against its existence; but this again is negative reasoning, and indeed begging the question somewhat in the mere choice of sites.

In any case, a certain body of information *has* been accumulated which, taken as a whole, somewhat does confirm the idea that the Norsemen went beyond the Greenland settlements. And some of the archaeological evidence can be localized to areas covered by the maps.

First, the question of how far north along the Greenland coast the Norsemen attained must be addressed. Start by considering the existence of known Norse cairns containing the rune stone from 1333 shown in Plate 12, found on the small island of Kingigtorssuaq at 72°58′ N., over halfway up the west coast of Greenland. This is just in the neighborhood where I have suggested that the post-Vinland Norsemen had their first contact with the Eskimos around 1266. I surmise that such cairns were set up by the Norsemen to denote places where they desired to meet and trade with the Eskimos (presumably for meat, skins and Eskimo soapstone products). To my knowledge, no excavations have been made as of this writing to look for evidence of such trade on Kingigtorssuaq. Nevertheless, just a mile east on the tiny island of Inugsuk, which also bears a cairn,

Therkel Mathiassen has uncovered an Eskimo settlement which contained many evidences of commerce with the Norsemen.[1] Several of the Norse objects found in this otherwise completely Eskimo deposit, shown in Plate 8, are of the nature of trinkets, presumably traded in the same way that later traders bartered with glass beads. These include a tooled spinning top, a wooden cameo carving of a Norsewoman's face and two figurines in characteristic Norse garb. (A nearby island, Kitsorsauq, yielded a third Norse figurine without digging. Mathiassen suggests that these were made by Eskimos in imitation of Norsemen they had seen.) Another object found, of no apparent value to the Eskimos except as a trinket, was a tiny piece of woven cloth. This is a reminder of a scene centuries earlier when Thorfinn Karlsefni's Saga described trade with the Skraelings in Vinland for cloth:

They had dark unblemished skins to exchange for the cloth, and were taking a span's length of cloth for a skin, and this they tied around their heads. In this way the trade continued for a while, then when the cloth began to run short they cut it up so that it was no broader than a fingerbreadth, but the Skraelings gave just as much for it, or more.

The wonder of woven cloth is such a luxury that in later years even the Greenlanders themselves considered it one of their most treasured imports, according to Zeno.

While these finds are apparently strictly trinkets, Mathiassen also uncovered evidence of genuine Norse cultural influence on the Eskimos. He found an alloyed iron hand hammer as well as several fragments of harpoon heads of damascened steel, which could only have been supplied by the Norsemen. He found many harpoon shafts with slots so narrow that they could only have been meant for such steel heads. Thus, to the extent of using steel at least, the Inugsuk Eskimos were actually dependent on trade with the Norsemen. While they could not assimilate the technology of steelmaking, they were able to adapt several other Norse technologies to their own capabilities. Thus Mathiassen found saws made out of baleen and oval-bowled spoons of antler. The most amazing of all the finds were coopered tubs made by the original Inugsuk Eskimos. He found a tub, complete and intact, as well as staves all the way to the bottom of the deposit, showing that the Eskimos had quickly learned the highly useful art of coopering. (The Eskimos used the tubs as containers for hide tanning.) In addition, the Eskimos seem to have copied several Norse ornamental design features on otherwise strictly Eskimo objects.

The fact that this place, Inugsuk, is located just at the place where I have surmised the initial meeting of the Greenlanders with the Eskimos (outside of original Vinland), at the middle of Greenland's west coast, is significant. It suggests a way of explaining the degree to which the inhabitants had absorbed Norse culture. That is, that the contact of the cultures could have been more prolonged here than elsewhere. However, much farther north, at the very northwesternmost corner of Greenland, on the endpaper map, Erik Holtved has found several Eskimo sites that show at least as great an amalgamation of Norse and Eskimo culture.[2] The characteristics of these excavations show that an entirely new Eskimo culture group had sprung up of widespread geographical distribution which, in fact, superseded the old Thule culture in many places. After the place of its original discovery, the new Eskimo culture has been named the Inugsuk culture. From the Eskimo side, the primary feature characterizing the Inugsuk culture is

its widespread use in toolmaking of the aforementioned
horny substance, baleen, from the upper jaws of whales,
and an attendant increase in whale hunting. From the
Norse side, the Inugsuk culture remains in northwesternmost Greenland revealed just as much Norse influence as
those on the island of Inugsuk itself. There were large
numbers of baleen saws, coopered tubs and a heavy dependence on iron blades. As Holtved points out, there are
deposits of meteoric iron not far from Thule which the
Eskimos could have hammered into blades themselves. However, he has not reported the results of standard recom-
mended tests taken to determine the layer structure, which
would resolve the question. Spectral tests showed that most
of the iron recovered was not meteoric, but instead apparently industrially refined. There were, as well, a number of objects of ancient industrial copper and brass,
a knife handle inlaid with highly purified lead, and a
Norse iron nail. As typified in Plate 9, there were wooden
boxes of various kinds with characteristic Norse structural
features, a variety of deep-bowled spoons and ladles, and
a strictly Norse spoon case. But of all the Norse trinkets
found, perhaps the most fascinating are two chessmen and
a fragment of chain-mail armor. The standard fragment of
cloth and spinning top were found, along with Norse figurines. And more in the nature of luxuries than trinkets were
a fine-toothed Norse comb and a Norse strainer funnel.

Holtved's excavations brought to light another highly
important feature in the ruins which might be of Norse
origin—the remains of rectangular houses and fireplaces.
The attitude toward these relics has been somewhat controversial, and Holtved has attempted to attribute them to
Eskimo developments. Indeed, the "Dorset culture" which
preceded the Thule culture is supposed by some to have

used rectangular houses, but this has not yet been firmly
proved.[3] Other writers have argued that these rectangular
houses are Norse influences. It is in truth difficult to say
whether any remnants of Dorset culture survived the Thule
invasion and coexisted with the Norsemen,[4] but the consensus is that it seems unlikely. In one such square building
on a small island now called Ruin Island, Holtved found
a fragment of Norse cloth and a Norse iron spearhead. The
building was apparently used as a storehouse for various
objects made of baleen, most of whose functions could be
identified. One group of objects that seemed to have no
imaginable function in the Eskimo culture, shown in Plate
10, was a number of thick lines of baleen fiber with heavy
knots and lashings. Until some conceivable Eskimo function
is found for them, it is tempting to speculate that they were
intended for rigging on Norse ships. Ruin Island has no
regular Norse cairn, but at its highest point there is an
artifically placed large boulder that can be seen from a
great distance. Whether this boulder was erected by man
or by the glacier cannot be decided from Holtved's published report.

That the Norse culture reached these northernmost parts
of Greenland directly rather than through intra-Eskimo
trade is proven, if further proof is needed, by the con-
stancy of concentration of Norse artifacts in the finds. If an
Eskimo trade chain had brought the artifacts up from the
established Norse settlements, one would expect to find the
concentration heavy near the settlements and sharply de-
creasing toward the far North. Instead, Mathiassen's excavations of Inugsuk sites right around the ruins of the Eastern Settlement at Julianehaab[5] have shown a concentration
of Norse objects not much greater than that on Ruin Island,
1500 miles northward. The only way the Norse influence

on the Eskimos could possibly have been distributed so
evenly is that the highly mobile Norsemen exerted their
influence simultaneously at all points once they discovered
the Eskimos in 1266. Indeed, a Norse ruin just below Svartenhuk, on the endpaper map, which was previously considered a bear trap, is now believed to be a church or
chapel,[6] presumably for the benefit of Norsemen on long
trips.

It is no wonder that Ivar Bardsson thought the Western
Settlement was showing too much friendship to the pagan
Eskimos. From the Western Settlement the Norse trade
routes to Europe were highly impractical compared to the
Norse trade routes to the Eskimos; and for a few iron
blades and trinkets a Norseman could probably get a whole
season's supply of frozen meat. The bargain the Norsemen
could drive probably was no less favorable to them than
that which modern man drives with the Eskimo for the pelt
of the blue fox. If the impact of the cross-cultural meeting
on the Eskimo culture is noticeable, its impact on the Norse
culture must also have been observable. Ivar Bardsson observed it, but not as an anthropologist. The Eastern Settlement held onto its European values somewhat longer, but
it is ultimately from the Eastern Settlement by way of Zeno's
description that we have some documented notion of how
the meeting affected the Norse culture—the adoption of the
kayak and Eskimo house-building methods, probably accompanied by the acquiring of Eskimo hunting techniques
as well. In fact, it is just these cultural features we should
expect the Norsemen to have adopted as they shifted
from husbandry to hunting. The massive stone structures
of the Norse settlements, especially, would have been highly
impractical to duplicate as bases for hunting parties or as
temporary quarters for a trading mission to the far north.

Just as Eskimos frequently move into and recondition previously abandoned stone igloos rather than build a new one from scratch, similarly it seems fair to assume that the Norsemen made use of previous Eskimo habitations on trading voyages. In reconditioning them for habitability they would have soon enough learned the Eskimos' special theory of construction and their great efficiency. The Eskimos themselves would have been more than happy to assist them in every way, and Eskimo folk tales show that the Eskimos looked upon the Norsemen as a pitiable lot who didn't know how to deal properly with the Arctic unless aided.

As the Norsemen rebuilt or reconditioned previously abandoned Eskimo dwellings for their own temporary use in the far north, it is almost certain that they would have added a separate fireplace or "kitchen" for preparing food in the manner with which they were familiar. If the previous dwelling had deteriorated to such an extent, however, that it was simply a handy collection of usable stones, then the most likely form for their new construction would, of course, be the Norsemen's own familiar form, rectangular. When the trading was finished and the Norsemen departed, the Eskimos would be left with a perfectly good rectangular construction that they could well make use of themselves. (There are many cases in the Western Settlement itself where Eskimos built on rectangular Norse foundations after they were abandoned.[7])

Thus, the alternate occupation of such sites by the two different cultures would on the one hand have influenced the cultures themselves and on the other hand left a cultural deposit that is a mixture of the two. Thus, in particular, it cannot be said with certainty whether the Norse "trinkets" found in Eskimo ruins were left there by Eskimos or

by the Norsemen themselves. Most likely it was a combination of contributions from the two. If the possession of Norse
trinkets had some status value for the Eskimos, then one
would expect similar status value for the Eskimos from
copying the Norsemen's rectangular buildings and fireplaces. In any case, the preservation of these forms would
have had the practical value of encouraging the Norsemen
to return again soon to where they knew they could find
comfortable accommodations. It is entirely conceivable that
such a process was also behind the later development of
Eskimo communal houses of larger rectangular form. The
Norsemen, at any rate, were well known to the Eskimos all
along the west coast of Greenland.

During one of the early modern attacks on the arctic ice
with steam vessels, an expedition was progressing northward along the eastern shore of Ellesmere Island, on the
endpaper map. Halfway up this coast on tiny Washington
Irving Island the party found a summit occupied by the
two cairns in Plate 11, which "were much too old" to have
been built by any modern explorers and must have been
Norse.

They were built of conglomerate and rested on a similar base,
which in one case had become undermined by the natural
crumbling away of the rock, and in doing so had destroyed a part
of the cairn. Lichens which had spread from stone to stone also
proved that they were of great age. They contained no record
whatever.[8]

From previous experience with Norse cairns we might expect to find some Inugsuk settlement nearby. To my knowledge, no excavations have been undertaken in this vicinity.
Nevertheless, on another small islet about twenty-five miles
southwest from there, another member of the expedition

found a tiny stone construction, now known to be Norse, which he drew as in Plate 13 and described as follows:

It consisted of four stones piled together like a miniature "Druid altar," so as to form a chamber large enough to shelter a nest. Generations of eider duck had been hatched in it in peace and security since the last wild hunter left the shore.[9]

The discoverer's apparent presumption that Eskimos had set up this nesting place to trap eider ducks has been proven to be incorrect.[10] In fact, the Norsemen from Greenland to Scandinavia have built such "eider houses" since time immemorial for just the opposite purpose—to protect eider nests and periodically harvest eider down for their quilts.[11] The presence of such eider houses signals not only the presence of Norsemen but, in particular, the presence of Norsemen during the high period of Greenland culture before the dispersal. For once the Greenlanders began to lose their settled European culture with its spinning wheels and looms, as they became hunting nomads, they would no longer have been able to provide the luxury of lightweight outer shells for eider-down quilts, and would have had to rely simply on animal skins, which are much heavier. At this point, the lightweight advantage of using eider down would have been lost. The natural place to find such eider houses is on tiny off-shore islands where the nests were safe from wolves and the Norsemen had easy access to them with their ships. In fact, just such tiny islands have yielded finds of more eider houses in two different localities farther south. One locality was around Buchanan Bay in east-central Ellesmere Island with about twelve eider houses discovered.[12] In this same locality Herman Simmons explored a deserted Eskimo village, which he calls "Eskimo-

polis," and found it to contain two perfectly rectangular
dwelling houses which include what appears to be a separate fireplace. These rectangular dwellings were apparently
built on the ruins of former round houses.[13]

The second more southerly locality, on the endpaper
map, in which eider houses were found was at the very
inner end of Jones Sound, between Ellesmere Island and
the next island southward, Devon.[14] The innermost find
was on tiny Devil Island, right in the narrow strait between
Jones Sound and the open water on the west side of Devon
and Ellesmere. The Norsemen who tended this nest had to
be wary of the strong tidal currents here, for they were
working right in the feared "indrawing channels" of Norse
lore. Nevertheless, this locality seems to have been a center
of major activity for the Norsemen, for nearby Gunnar
Isachsen discovered two round cairns of Norse construction:

The cairns were 1.5 meters [5 feet] high and built of flat but
small stones. They had dimension, form and material completely
unlike all other constructions of Eskimos which the expedition
encountered.[15]

The Isachsen brothers have pointed out the seemingly
curious fact that Norse cairns usually occur in pairs. In this
case, the cairns may have defined a direction line* to
some place of importance, and it is unfortunate that those
who have observed them have not reported their relative
situation and orientation. For, in fact, before the modern
construction of roads in Iceland, cairns were used to mark
the easiest overland routes from one settlement to an-

* A Norse site excavated by Ingstad also has a pair of cairns.[16]
There were three cairns forming an equilateral triangle on Kingigtorssuaq, but the one with the rune stone was much larger than the
other two so that a direction could still be implied.

other.[17] Whether or not the Norsemen had settlements around these islands, there can be no doubt about their active presence there.

The earliest map involving the Smaller Misunderstanding which can be identified with complete confidence is a map showing Baffin Island. When one looks for archaeological traces of the Norsemen on Baffin Island, however, he finds neither cairns nor eider houses. Perhaps, nevertheless, this possible Norse exploration without occupation is what should be expected here. The east coast of Baffin Island is a particularly barren and uninviting stretch of land, in most places bare rock devoid of even tundra, plunging sharply into the sea. The Eskimos themselves have largely avoided this coast. To the Norsemen it would not have represented a place to be exploited, but rather a place to circumnavigate. (Except for one important resource: white falcons. The towering cliffs are a favorite habitat for the falcons, and were probably discovered long before contact with the Eskimos created a desire to get around them. Most of the white falcons seen in Greenland would have been observed to have flown in from the west, i.e., Baffin Island.)

Perhaps it is significant that map making in connection with the Norsemen has as its first definitely identifiable specimen this roadblock to trade with the Eskimos farther west. The search for ways around Baffin Island must have had its parallels with the later search for ways around America. It is, of course, the members of the Western Settlement who would have been primarily engaged in this activity. Soon enough, they would have realized the impracticality of going all the way north along Greenland and then coming south along Ellesmere, to avoid any "middle ice" of Baffin Bay, and would have sought a more

direct summer route across Davis Strait. Regardless of this,
if one sails up the east coast of Baffin Island looking for a
passage westward he eventually comes to the inviting Pond
Inlet at the northeastern corner of Baffin. Here on the
south shore of Pond Inlet, Mathiassen uncovered a piece of
cast copper alloy near the bottom of an Eskimo deposit
under archaeological conditions making it difficult to attribute the object to modern man.[18] If this was a trace
left by the Norsemen, it must have been a result of contact
less intensive than that which resulted in the previously
mentioned Inugsuk culture amalgam of Norse and Thule,
for most other Eskimo remains on the spot were clearly of
the Thule culture. Nevertheless, much evidence was found
of metal blades and weapon heads, which may conceivably
indicate an early phase of transition to Inugsuk culture.
These traces constitute justification at least for entertaining
a possibility of a Norse origin of the maps of Baffin Island.

While the specific meanings of many of the artifacts discussed so far allow room for clarification, there can be no
doubt about their overall meaning when looked at together.
What they strongly imply is that the Norsemen from the
settlements in southern Greenland sailed, and frequently
sailed, all the way to the northern end of Greenland, and
then sailed all around the upper part of Baffin Bay. Most
importantly, it is obvious that the Norsemen got along completely peaceably with the Eskimos, and both shared intensive cultural contacts with each other.

These facts leave little room for doubt that the Norse
Greenlanders were in a position to learn map making from
the Eskimos and, at the same time, to develop a curiosity
about the Eskimo lands to the west.

CHAPTER 8

The Norse Dispersal into Canada

There is just one regularly usable sea portal to the central
Arctic: Lancaster Sound, between Baffin Island and its
northern neighbor, Devon Island. Can any archaeological
evidence be provided that the Norsemen went through this
portal and were thus enabled to map the central Arctic?
The answer as of this writing must be an unsatisfying
"maybe." The inconclusiveness of the situation is attributa-
ble to the relative dearth of excavations in the central
Arctic and the large number of surface discoveries that cannot be reliably classified without further excavations. The
modern Icelandic scholar Jon Duason and his followers have
compiled an extensive list of surface finds which seem to
them more Norse than Eskimo, but their theories are far
from universally accepted.* A summary of these theories is
given in English by Trygvie Oleson in his *Early Voyages.*

Since archaeology is unable at present to answer conclusively the question of whether the Norsemen entered the

* Particularly unacceptable is their tenet that the Thule culture resulted from a genetic and cultural fusion of the Dorset Eskimos and
the Norsemen.

central Arctic, one is still left without confirmation of the Norse origin of the maps of that region. But one still seeks such confirmation. This situation requires turning temporarily away from deductive reasoning to explore a more circumstantial means of inquiry. To this end, several apparently divergent circumstances must be examined.

It must be realized that any voyage from the Greenland settlements to the back side of Baffin Island, enabling map making of the central Arctic, would have been truly a major voyage—in every way more difficult than the voyage to Iceland. For the Greenlanders to have come here and back again on a summer voyage for simple trade with the Eskimos is actually out of the question. Even polar bear or falcon hunting this far from the settlements cannot be justified. The only motive that could have justified the presence of the Norsemen in the central Arctic is survival.

One would not normally think of a flight to the central Arctic as a means of survival. But, paradoxically, with the onset of the so-called Little Ice Age in the fourteenth century, hunting in the central Arctic offered more chance of survival than dairy farming in Greenland.[1] The nature and causes of the Little Ice Age are much in debate, but its existence is unquestionable.[2] During its peak in the fifteenth and sixteenth century the Baltic Sea froze over from shore to shore and terrible storms wracked Europe. The glaciers in the Alps, Iceland, Scandinavia and the Rockies noticeably advanced.[3] Such climatic changes do not suddenly burst upon the world, however, but rather approach by almost imperceptible degrees. In conducting their affairs on a daily or annual basis, humans have a way of responding to such imperceptible changes without realizing they are doing so. Specifically as the climate first deteriorated in the Western Settlement four hundred miles north of the Eastern, the dairy farmers of the Western would have found themselves occasionally spending more time than usual hunting in Nordrsetur, their name for the game-teeming northern half of Greenland's west coast, to make up for an early hay-killing frost. Eventually some would even have placed as much emphasis on equipping their ships for Nordrsetur as on acquiring new cattle. The more southerly Eastern Settlement meanwhile would have been doing dairy farming as usual, with neither yet fully realizing that this divergent cultural pattern had already been set.

By the time of Ivar Bardsson's visit in the 1340s the Western Settlement perhaps realized these changes in its own life style, but the Eastern Settlement still expected the Western men to be dairying. The Eastern Settlement's subsequent ostracism of the renegade Western must have accelerated the Western's dispersal and dependence on hunting, for the Western could now no longer obtain the Eastern's industrial products or, through it, the products of Europe. While contact between the Western and Eastern Settlements was probably never *completely* severed, one must nevertheless expect there to have been a decline in the later Western Settlement of what I might call the classical Greenland-European culture. The height of the economy behind this culture was characterized by extensive dairy farming based on the ability of cattle to convert the alpine grasses of Greenland into edible milk protein (and perhaps some beef). This economic base was supplemented primarily by caribou hunting in the Western Settlement,[4] and frequently by the hunting of marine mammals—primarily the harp seal in the Eastern Settlement.[5] (These were not really hunted, but rather "harvested" at certain times of the year as they conveniently migrated past the settlements.)

While farming conditions deteriorated in the Western

Settlement, the residents supplemented their diet with meat easily procured locally; but when farming eventually became impossible a "supplement" was no longer enough. When they became completely dependent on hunting, it would have made no sense to continue residing in the Western Settlement. Rather it would have been sensible to move to the most abundant source of game known to them: the central Arctic. Every year saw the migration of unbelievable herds of caribou across ice from the mainland to the Arctic Archipelago and back again.[6] When hundreds of thousands of caribou[7] are on the move they pay little attention to human hunters, and a strategically placed Norseman at the edge of the travel way could have harvested a year's supply of meat for his family in a short season.[8] While the Thule Eskimos were a coastal people depending primarily upon sea mammals, they nevertheless used caribou skin clothing, and they gladly consumed the meat of any caribou that came within range of their camps. As the Thules migrated through this region they could not have helped but observe the caribou spectacle. Then the Norsemen would have learned about it from them in Greenland.

If this Norse evacuation of the Western Settlement actually occurred, as Ivar Bardsson suggests it did, then it must be certain that for all practical purposes they were then cut off from the Eastern Settlement and were then essentially compatriots of the Eskimos. For practical purposes it must be expected that their primary language came to be Eskimo, their method of housebuilding, Eskimo and their clothing, Eskimo. This has been the case with all but the most recent modern explorers who entered the area, and indeed it is the only way to survive in the high Arctic, short of continuous airlifts of modern equipment and supplies. If these ghosts from the Western Settlement had the same urge to survive

as all other peoples, then they must have taken on an Eskimo way of life. Indeed, even if the "Little Ice Age" were
not severe enough to have totally disrupted their farming, it
may well have been that once they had learned the Eskimo
way of dealing with the Arctic, they found Arctic caribou
hunting an easier way of life than Greenland dairy farming.
Once contact was established with the central Arctic caribou
herds, it may well have been that the ultimate exodus was
by choice rather than necessity. Caribou are known to be
among the most easily killed of all game animals,[9] and this
fact may have provided enough temptation for the already
isolated members of the Western Settlement to cut their ties
completely.

If any Norsemen did move to the central Arctic, then one
must expect them to have undergone a change in culture
(in the strict anthropological sense) as well as in economy.
The implements of nomadic hunting are not the same as the
implements of settled husbandry, and clearly neither is the
way of life. In particular, to look for widespread evidences
of the high Norse culture in the central Arctic as evidence
of their presence is unrealistic. In fact, as survival became
the main concern, one must expect that there was a marked
decline from the old relatively luxurious culture.

Nevertheless, they were still genetically Norsemen, still
probably had some occasional contact with the Eastern Settlement and still would have sought to retain wherever useful the technical aspects of their historic culture. One can
speculate with reasonable confidence about some elements
whose retention would have proved valuable.

The mobility provided by the Norse ships would have
been most useful in following the migrations of various game
from the mainland to the archipelago or from one seacoast
to another. While Eskimo sledges would have provided a

more practical mobility over a greater part of the year, a certain momentum of cultural habit could have been expected to delay the complete abandonment of the use of sailing ships while the ex-members of the Western Settlement sought hunting grounds to the west. Thus, one might expect to find traces of Norse ships in the central Arctic at least from a relatively brief period. Such traces are understandably difficult to be found even if they are present, for the discovery of underwater relics is a rare breakthrough even in Scandinavia itself. Nevertheless, various apparently non-Eskimo stone structures have been found in the central Arctic which some writers believe to have been winter shelters for dry-docked Norse ships.[10] The technical discussion of these finds is beyond the scope of this book, and it would seem that in the archaeologist's shovel lies the only hope of definitely resolving the question.

With regard to another technical aspect of the Norse culture, the central Arctic offers a surprising bonus—metal. The established Norse technique of smelting metal from its ore could not have been widely practiced in the absence of the permanent settlement necessary to maintain such an industry, but the central Arctic has several locations where pure native copper appears on the surface of the earth.[11] Large nodules of copper are to be found in an area, on the endpaper map, near the mouth of the Coppermine River at the western end of Coronation Gulf as well as around Bathurst Inlet at its eastern end, and Eskimos report copper nodules the size of a man at the inner end of Prince Albert Sound on Victoria Island.[12] The value such deposits would have had for the wandering Norsemen was obviously great. While the ancient Thule Eskimos who passed through the area apparently did not learn to make use of the copper, the modern inhabitants of the area are called Copper Eskimos because of their use of the metal. The inadequately explained[13] question of how they learned to use the copper to make their implements might be answered if it could be shown conclusively that the Norsemen were in the area.

A strange surface discovery in the area of the Copper Eskimos is a number of cairns of apparently non-Eskimo type.[14] In reporting these, Diamond Jenness does not describe their construction explicitly but accepts the description "piles of stone similar to the cairns that the shepherds of Scotland built for landmarks." The Viking influence in Scotland is well known,[15] but the idea of Eskimos setting off property limits with landmarks is unheard of. It is unfortunate that the explorers who have seen these cairns have not published photographs of them or described their signs of antiquity.

A subject that goes hand in hand with the question of mutual interaction of the Norse and Eskimo cultures after a hypothetical permanent move to the central Arctic is the question of interracial mixing. Ever since Viking times the Norsemen have left their genes behind at places they visited, and the question is not one of whether or not mixing took place. Rather, the question is whether it took place to such an extent that the ultimate disappearance of the Norsemen can be attributed to their complete absorption into the Eskimo race. When two different races occupy the same territory they tend to maintain their racial separateness so long as they maintain their cultural and economic separateness. But once the different cultures have become amalgamated, many of the taboos against intermixing disappear. In 1942 Knud Fischer-Möller reported the finding in a Greenland church graveyard of two skeletons having features that prove that mixing was not unheard of even in the settlements.[16] The political infusion of Germanic studies

during the second quarter of the twentieth century may
have prevented some Teutonic scholars from considering this
question rationally, but before that time there were many
adherents to the theory that the Norsemen had been completely absorbed into the Eskimo race. As early as 1776, an
Icelandic scholar propounded the theory of racial absorption, and around the turn of the twentieth century this came
to be known as the Nansen Theory.[17]

The trouble with this theory was that it was based primarily upon inductive speculation rather than upon much explicit evidence. Then in the early 1900s a discovery by the
adventurer Klengenberg and investigations by the anthropologist Vilhjalmur Stefansson brought to light the apparent
presence of European genes among a small group of Eskimos
who had previously been isolated from all contact with
modern white man. This tribe, known as the Haneragmiut,
lived at the heart of the region I have just been discussing,
in southwest Victoria Island. Entries in Stefansson's diary
include descriptions such as:

There are three men here whose beards are almost the color of
mine, and who look like typical Scandinavians . . . men with
abundant three-inch-long beards* . . . The faces and proportions of the body remind of "stocky," sunburned, but naturally
fair Scandinavians . . . One woman, of about twenty, has the
delicate features one sees in some Scandinavian girls, and that
I have seen in only one of the half-white girls to the westward
(Mackenzie River), and in her to a less degree than here.[18]

That such copy would be overplayed by newspapers is
completely understandable, and these people were immediately dubbed the "Blond" Eskimos. Soon Stefansson was

* Pure Eskimos have almost no facial hair, and their word *Kabluna*
for Caucasian man means "long-beard."

being confronted with accusations of fraud no less vehement than those that met Stanley when he announced his finding of Livingston. Even Stefansson's professional stature as an anthropologist was brought into question when a specialist in ethnology on a later expedition, Jenness, was apparently unable to locate this tribe.[19] Furthermore, Jenness tried to explain any such characteristics which might exist as pathological deformities,[20] and noted the absence of any European skeletal features. The controversy then quickly escalated when Jenness' own scientific method[21] as well as the accuracy of his observational reports[22] were called into question.

Certainly to use Stefansson's observations as an argument for the ultimate absorption of the Norsemen into the Eskimos is, in any case, going too far, for there is not available any dependable knowledge of the relative population levels of either the Norsemen or the Eskimos at the time. Even to use the "Blond" Eskimos as an argument for the very presence of Norsemen in the central Arctic is going too far without more agreement among anthropologists. The entire subject of Eskimo anthropology is a highly factionalized and controversial one, and a not-too-out-of-date survey of the relevant literature has been given by Maksim Levin.[23] In any case, modern studies of genetic drift make it clear that one must hesitate about jumping to conclusions when dealing with such small populations.[24]

But eventually Jenness as well as many other investigators, including Stefansson again, found similar facial characteristics, including blue eyes, to a less marked degree in scattered individuals throughout the central Arctic. If Norse ancestry is truly indicated thereby, it should not be surprising that it is manifested primarily in facial characteristics rather than skeletal characteristics. A group such as the

Norsemen trying to maintain its racial identity in spite of
absorption may have, over the generations, tended by what
I might call "un-natural selection" to hold onto such easily
observed facial features. That is, those who considered light
hair or eyes as part of their heritage might have sought out
mates with similar facial characteristics, ignoring the potential mate's skeletal heritage. (One cannot, of course, expect the preservation of actual blond hair in the light of the
dominance of black hair.) Stefansson's report seems to imply that the "Blond" Eskimos thought of their features in a
positive way rather than as pathologies. Perhaps the most
conclusive commentary on the subject was made by Wissler, who pointed out the extremely low probability of any
random occurrence, by genetic drift, of several such European characteristics simultaneously in single individuals.[25]

Some enthusiasts may find encouragement in their belief
that these people were descendants of the Norsemen from
an east-central Arctic Eskimo folk tale that describes a
strange group of people the Eskimos called "Tunit." The
suggestion is that the Tunit were actually Norsemen. The
Tunit legend relates to the time before the modern culture
of Eskimos from west of Baffin Island came to be caribou
hunters.

It was the Tunit who first found the places where the caribou
crossed the waters, and they built fences in various parts of the
country and thus compelled the animals to follow certain paths
so that while on land they could be hunted with the bow and
arrow from blinds or pursued in kayaks at the crossing places.[26]

Those who believe the legendary Tunit were Thule Eskimos[27] rather than Norsemen would have difficulty explaining how this coastal, sea-mammal-oriented culture could

have been the originator of inland caribou hunting in its finest details.[28] Another quite glaring discrepancy, which such advocates overlook, is that while an important theme of many versions of the legends is the great height of the Tunit individuals relative to modern Eskimos, the definitive report on the Thule skeletal remains shows no difference in stature between modern Eskimos and the bearers of the Thule culture.[29] On the other hand, an entirely different culture of Eskimos which preceded the Thules, the above-mentioned Dorset culture Eskimos, has been also suggested as a candidate for the legendary Tunit.[30] While many characteristics of the Dorsets, such as the lack of dogs and bows, favor this identification, not all aspects of this culture are yet completely known. In particular, no investigator has shown any evidence that Dorset Eskimos had any different physical size from the Thules or the present Eskimos.[31] The tendency of some writers to base their knowledge of the Dorset culture on the descriptions in the Tunit legends is obviously circular. But whatever the origins of the Tunit legends, it would seem natural for them to serve as depositories for lore about both the Dorsets and the Norsemen, and that such legends later would have been embellished by modern Eskimos with more recent memories of the Thule culture. The Eskimo legend also says that the Tunit were skilled at musk ox hunting and were bold bear hunters.[32] This is typically un-Thule, and it is also difficult to make a case for any extensive land hunting done by the Dorsets.[33] The discovery by the Norsemen of musk oxen in the central Arctic, which did not occur in their part of Greenland, would have been a further attraction of the area to them because musk oxen taste more nearly like domestic beef than any other Arctic animal. The Netsilik version of the Tunit

legend contains another passage that is much more accurately descriptive of the Norsemen than any Eskimos:

In contrast to the present population [as well as the previous
Thule or Dorset populations], they loved the sea when it was not
covered with ice.[34]

All Eskimos, of course, prefer an ice-covered sea which offers
them easy and fast transportation with sledges, dog-drawn
or not, and, before the advent of firearms, easy seal hunting at breathing holes. The nautical background of the
Norsemen would have predisposed them to the opposite, to
an ice-free sea, just as was the case with the modern European explorers who preceded Stefansson.[35] Finally, the same
sources that supplied the above quotes also mention that the
language of the Tunit was a different dialect from that of
the central Eskimos, and examples are given. Rasmussen has
shown that this Tunit dialect is the dialect of Greenland,[36]
which is just what one would expect from a Norseman who
learned his Eskimo at home among the Greenland Eskimos.

Jenness has described an old stone hut at the western end
of Coronation Gulf,[37] shown in Plate 14, similar to several
finds by Stefansson in the central Arctic.[38] Several writers
have described a modern Eskimo use of these structures as
fox "tower traps," where the door is closed off, the top opened or fitted with a delicately balanced lid, and bait placed
inside. However, that they were originally constructed for
that purpose is unthinkable, since, first, a fox can reach the
top to get himself trapped only with great difficulty, and
second, the door is so large that a trapped fox might easily
escape when the door is opened to remove him. Another use
to which these structures has been put by modern Eskimos

is in storing caches of meat for possible emergency use in bad seasons. However, the standard Eskimo meat cache is simply a pile of meat covered over with stones to protect it from predators, and the original building of these permanent structures for such a purpose would have been completely contrary to the Eskimos' nomadic existence. According to Oleson, however, precisely such structures were constructed for food storage by the Norsemen in Iceland and Greenland.[39] Jenness' Eskimos told him that the example he saw was not built by Eskimos, and the example Stefansson saw was claimed to have been built by the Tunit. Stefansson reported a particular concentration of such structures in the part of Victoria Island between Prince Albert Sound and Minto Inlet,[40] which is traditionally the copper-bearing area of Victoria Island. In a completely different area, Canadian anthropologist Thomas E. Lee found such structures in proximity with "eider house" nests,[41] and he asserts they are large enough for a man to lie down in.[42] All of these circumstances point strongly to a Norse origin of these huts.

If the Norsemen indeed occupied arctic Canada, then they were in a position not only to originate the maps of the central Arctic, but also to make trips to Alaska, where another group of maps had its origin. I believe that the evidence I am about to present shows that such trips were made, but before finally coming to such a conclusion it will be necessary to dispel some very hard evidence to the contrary. Namely, from Alaska comes apparent evidence that the map sequence westward I have referred to in Chapter 5 might have been of Eskimo origin. For, the most advanced and most recent examples of the Thule culture have been discovered not in Greenland but in Alaska, where modern Eskimos maintained to recent times a culture similar to ad-

vanced Thule.[43] Many anthropologists have explained this
situation by postulating a "back-wave" of Thule migration
from east to west in relatively recent centuries.[44] Obviously,
such a migration would correlate very well with the time
and sequence of the maps I have discussed, and might be
considered as evidence for demonstrating a strictly Eskimo
origin of all the maps.

When the situation is examined further, however, it
becomes apparent that no rational motivation for such a
migration can be given in strictly Eskimo terms.[45] The
Thules had just previously finished an extremely long migration from Alaska to Greenland, and now, for no apparent
reason, this *ad hoc* theory would call for them to have
turned around and marched back—with great speed, at
that. If the Norsemen are brought into the picture, however,
the Thule back-wave's motivation might be postulated. As a
start, it may be noted that whenever two different cultures
are brought into contact, the people in each tend to divide
themselves into two groups—the progressives and the
reactionaries. An example of this polarization among the
Norsemen might be found in the Western Settlement's progressive attitude toward contact with the Eskimo and the
Eastern Settlement's at least temporarily reactionary attitude. Among the Eskimos the progressive element would
be represented by the Inugsuk culture, and the reactionary
element found in the Thule back wave. This explanation of
the Eskimo migration is *still* quite unsatisfactory, however,
for no amount of reaction would have required migration
all the way back to Alaska unless the Norsemen were right
on their heels. Nevertheless, there are theories that new
cultural contact can cause reaction at a distance through
the formation of cultural "ripples" which spread through
neighboring peoples.[46] The back wave might have been

THE NORSE DISPERSAL INTO CANADA [Chap. 8]   143

reacting not to the Norsemen but to the Inugsuks, and
later to those of their own number who were favorably
impressed by the Inugsuks, etc. Such a process should
indeed have the effect of repropagating a highly purified
Thule culture to the westward.

The trouble with this explanation is that, in order to fit
the facts, as soon as the Thules had reached Alaska they
would have had to immediately rush back eastward with
their map of Alaska to deliver it to the Norsemen in time
for meeting Clavus' publication date in Europe. There is
no record of such a double reverse wave. Furthermore,
the general nature of the westward migration does not
really seem to be reactionary, but contains many progressive
elements. The language dialect it spread is much more
closely related to the Greenland dialect than to the Alaskan
predecessor dialects, and its house forms are of the progressive Greenland type rather than the original form.[47]
Knowledge of the back wave is not yet sufficient to tell
if these Eskimos were dependent on metal blades, but evidently many of their harpoon shafts were prepared for
some type of very thin blade.[48] In many ways the culture
of the back wave seems like an advanced phase of Thule,
which never quite became Inugsuk.

This is, of course, just what one would expect if the
back wave was not retreating from the Norsemen but was,
instead, actually trying to follow them westward. While
attempting to follow them, the Eskimos would have been
unable to keep up with the mobility of the Norsemen,
and the sparse contact could well have resulted in a culture
somewhere in between old Thule and Inugsuk. Meanwhile,
the numbers of the Norsemen could have been so small and
their own culture become so Eskimoan as to camouflage
their traces.

The critic's hard evidence against the Norsemen in Alaska has been softened. Even the absolute lack of any archaeological traces of the Norsemen has had to yield to a circumstantial demonstration of the plausibility of their presence. But in this case "plausibility" may not be a strong enough word, for the presence of the Norsemen is the only way ever proposed of explaining these many curious features of the curious Thule back wave.

The time between the original contact of the Greenlanders with the Thule Eskimos in the late 1200s and the prototype for Clavus' Alaska map in the early 1400s was not much over a century. In this century the hypothetical travelers from the Western Settlement through arctic Canada may have experienced the beginnings of an absorption into the Eskimo culture and race, but they hardly could have forgotten their origin and historic ties with Scandinavia and Europe. Such Norse travelers through the central Arctic who had any geographical awareness whatsoever must have been certain (since they were participating in the Grand Misunderstanding) that they were heading westward along the northern coast of Asia. It may have occurred to some of them that they might, by continuing westward, eventually reach Scandinavia. Thus, the very identification of the Seward Peninsula with Scandinavia may have been established by such travelers much closer to the source of Clavus' map than Clavus himself.

Can the critical mind now be satisfied that the Norsemen indeed traveled westward through the Arctic? Everyone will have to answer for himself. I find myself anticipating that hard archaeological traces of the Norsemen in arctic Canada *will* eventually be forthcoming. With discoveries of oil and mineral deposits deep in the Canadian Arctic, it is rapidly being opened to travel, and doubtlessly many interesting archaeological answers will soon be found. Indeed, if the evidence is not to be destroyed by the eventually inevitable commercial inrush,[49] the answers will soon *have* to be found.

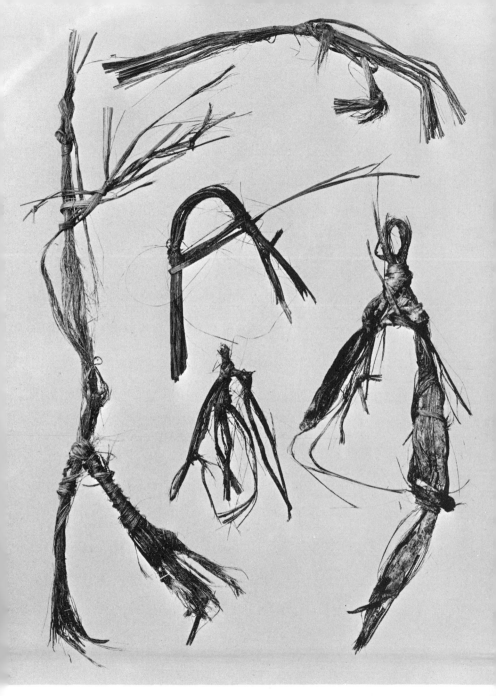

10. The Eskimos may have maintained nautical stations for the Norsemen. These heavy knots and lashings of baleen fiber, which are from the same Eskimo ruins that produced the chessmen, may have been rigging for Norse ships. This is discussed in Chapter 7.

11. After the Norsemen explored all the way northward in Greenland, they found the North American arctic islands just to Greenland's west, shown on the endpaper maps. This is a nineteenth-century explorer's drawing of Norse cairns he found there near Ellesmere Island.

12. Norse cairns sometimes contained inscribed stones describing their builders. This one, from a cairn in northerly Greenland, tells about a ship that was trapped there in pack ice and had to resort to sawing through the ice to break through.

13.　Typical Norse arctic wild-duck house used to lure ducks into building down-lined nests, which the Norsemen then removed for down quilts. This and many others were found near the straits between Ellesmere and Baffin islands which lead westward to the central Arctic. This geography may be seen on the endpaper maps. Chapter 8 shows how some Norsemen permanently migrated through these straits, gave up such luxuries as down quilts and lived like Eskimos there.

14.　Typical stone hut of probable Norse origin, many of which are found scattered throughout the archipelago north of Canada, shown on the endpaper maps. While Norsemen here lived like Eskimos, they kept some occasional contact with the settlements in Greenland.

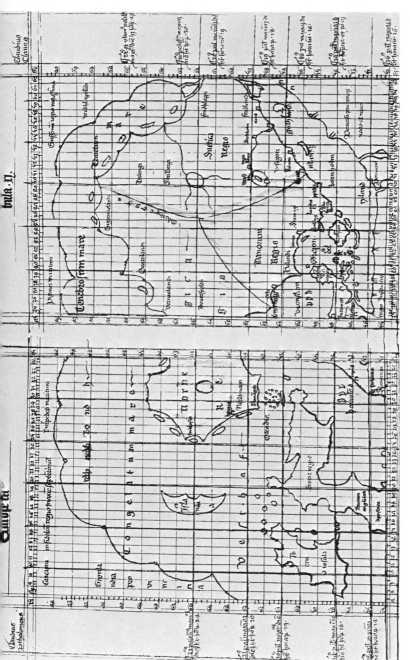

15. Medieval European map, claiming to represent Scandinavia, which has no resemblance at all to Scandinavia. It may be a misinterpretation of an actual Norse map of *Alaska*, as described in Chapter 5. Such maps, according to Chapter 5 and 6, may have motivated Columbus' voyages.

CHAPTER 9

Greenland's End and America's Beginnings

So far I have attempted the task of seeking archaeological and anthropological traces of Norse travel to the north and the west, and I have attributed those traces that do exist to a dispersal of the Western Settlement of Greenland. Now the question of whether there are any traces to corroborate the maps of lands south of Greenland remains to be discussed. To this purpose, it is useful to return one's attention to the more southerly Eastern Settlement at the period of its estrangement from the Western Settlement. Its circumstances must be examined. It is surmised that this estrangement was associated with a lack of understanding in the Eastern Settlement of the declining agricultural conditions of the Western Settlement and the attendant need there to turn to the Eskimo way of life. While the approach of the Little Ice Age was admittedly gradual, it was, nevertheless, only a matter of time until its effects also reached the agriculture of the Eastern Settlement. Thus, some forty years after Ivar Bardsson, one finds the entire Eastern Settlement unable to provide for the visit from Iceland of Björn Einarsson and his crew, and their dependence upon Eskimo assistance completely accepted. A decade later still, around 1395, Niccolò Zeno intimates an almost complete dependence of the settlement upon hunting, and with the dawn of the fifteenth century, European notices of civilized Greenland disappear.

Nevertheless, it would seem that the effect of the loss of agriculture on the Eastern Settlement was different from that on the Western Settlement. The Eastern Settlement was always the less provincial of the two, and more inclined to trade and keep contact with the European world. From the beginning, the Western Settlement was composed of those who wanted to go off by themselves exploring the rest of the world, those who wanted to be closer to the hunting grounds or those less able to cope with life in a more nearly urban Eastern Settlement. Thus, while the migration I have postulated for the Western Settlement seems rather natural for its inhabitants, it would seem less so for the Eastern Settlement. It would have been more natural for the Eastern Settlement to have gone to some lengths to maintain its integrity as a settlement and emphasize trade rather than hunting as a replacement for agriculture. This is just what is suggested by Zeno—his Greenland monks are dependent upon hunting done by the Eskimos and trade with the Eskimos for their food rather than hunt it themselves.

For the Eastern Settlement as a whole, trade with the Eskimos would naturally have been of some value, but another group of people would have provided an even more valuable occasional trade contact: namely, the previous members of the Western Settlement. Once the Eastern Settlement itself was forced to accept contact with the Eskimos there was no longer any basis for it to maintain its estrangement of the Western Settlement on those very grounds. However, by the time a re-establishment of contact might have been attempted in the fifteenth century, the old Western Settlement would have been dispersed (as was apparently already the case nearly a century before in Ivar Bardsson's time). This prior dispersal of the Western Settlement could now be only to the advantage of the Eastern Settlement. Instead of having to trade with the Eskimos, primarily for marine animals, they could occasionally trade with the wandering ex-residents of the Western Settlement for caribou and musk ox.

In fact, such a hypothesis provides a reasonable way of accounting for the sudden appearance described in Chapter 5 of the Quebec/Labrador Peninsula on European maps, in contrast to the prolonged century of development associated with the more northerly central Arctic maps. That is, one would expect to find a *gradual* development of the map if the people of the Eastern Settlement had surveyed such a map themselves in the process of a dispersal from their settlement, because they would have had to learn their way both in map making and exploring. On the other hand, one would expect to find a more sudden appearance of refined maps of the Quebec/Labrador Peninsula if the wanderers from the Western Settlement applied their now highly efficient techniques to finding a convenient hunting grounds for supplying the Eastern Settlement's trade needs. Indeed, the huge herds of caribou that annually crossed the ice, indicated on the endpapers, just before it melted and thus entered the Arctic Archipelago, also had an annual cycle of migration southward into the continent when the ice returned. This annual fluctuation between north and south would not have been discerned by the Eastern Settlement Norsemen sailing around the Greenland-Baffin Island area because the mountainous east coast of Baffin Island forms poor grazing land and keeps the caribou farther west. The dispersed Norsemen in the archipelago, however, after a suitable number of seasons of trying to follow the caribou south, would surely have discovered the easier access to the caribou of the Quebec/Labrador Peninsula via Hudson Strait. From then on, the Eastern Settlement would have been in a position to gain advantage from the trade. Exploration of the Quebec/Labrador Peninsula by the dispersed Norse traders would have been swift, and communication with Europe about this exploration, even if by way of pirates, would have been more direct than it was about the Western Settlement's dispersal in the north.

While there may have been a desire for more hard, noncontroversial evidence to definitely connect the Norsemen with the northerly maps, the appearance of magnetic compass variation in most of the southerly maps seems to provide the definite proof of a connection here. This is corroborated by a variety of archaeological finds. Recently, Thomas Lee excavated remains of a medieval European village, certainly Norse, at a strategic caribou grazing area in the Ungava Peninsula of northern Quebec.[1] Farley Mowat believes that certain obscure sagas refer to post-Vinland voyages into Ungava Bay.[2] Corroboration of more southerly voyages is claimed via information about the so-called "Schleswig Turkey." This strictly new-world temperate-zone bird appears in a twice-restored painting made originally in 1280 in the cathedral church in Schleswig, Germany. If the *ur* painting actually contained the bird,[3] then presumably the artist got his model through some Hanseatic contact with the Greenlanders.[4] Snail shells, carbon-dated to the pre-Columbian era, have been found in Nova Scotia and are of a species that was supposedly strictly native to European waters in pre-Columbian times.

The shells are now thought to have been introduced inadvertently into these American waters in the ballast of Norse ships.[5] The archaeologist Junius Bird has excavated Eskimo ruins in southern Labrador that contain Inugsuk-type influences,[6] and both Mallery[7] and Ingstad[8] have found actual Norse ruins in northern Newfoundland. Taken together, all this evidence leaves no question whatever that the Norsemen were in a position to have made the maps of eastern Canada from their own experience.

Thus, one might hope to address himself successfully to the question of how far south the Norsemen journeyed. Any such hope in terms of maps turns out to be unjustified, however, for the occurrence of the southward exploration apparently coincided with the cessation of recorded contact between Greenland and Europe. Therefore, there is no particular reason to believe that the southernmost map preserved (Nova Scotia) represents the southernmost attainment. Enthusiasts have convinced themselves they have found a Norse dry dock at Follins Pond, Massachusetts,[9] a Norse stone tower in Newport, Rhode Island,[10] rune stones in the Virginias[11] and even Oklahoma.[12]

However, anybody who would place the Norsemen so far south must first overcome some very strong objections.[13] Among these objections are the question regarding Norse interaction with hostile Indian tribes and the question of why the Norsemen would want to go so far south in the first place. It is a fallacy to assume that a natural desire of the Norsemen would have been to vacate the northlands in preference for more balmy latitudes. This kind of Temperate Zone chauvinism would also require the ancient Africans to have moved north from the Tropic Zone, which has not happened, or the Eskimos themselves to have moved southward. As long as people can make a living they tend to stay within an environment of maximum familiarity. As for the problem of hostile natives, Norse contact with the Eskimos was possible because the Eskimos would never band together to make joint reprisal for individually suffered Norse offenses. But with the Indians the case would have been entirely different. Considering the traditional Norse aggressiveness, the overwhelming majority of the Indians and their tendency to band together, it seems surprising that the Norse reached as far south as Nova Scotia, or even the Quebec/Labrador Peninsula, without being wiped out.

But evidently the ex-Vikings had now learned the value of diplomacy in place of aggressiveness. Even with firearms, Columbus found that diplomacy was a more successful way of dealing with the Indians than great companies of soldiers. It was later explorers who brought out the hostile aspect of the Indians by treating *them* hostilely.

Many writers have argued that positing a friendly interaction between the Norsemen and the Indians is a means of explaining the history of the game Lacrosse. This game was first taught to modern white man by the Algonkin Indians of the upper St. Lawrence valley. And it has many essential features that are identical to the essential features of the old Norse game of *knattleikr*. One of these features, that of paired opponents whose interaction may not be interfered with by other players, is so unique as to rule out the likelihood of simple coincidence in the genesis of the games. That it is actually one and the same game, taught to the Indians by the Norsemen, indeed does seem the most likely conclusion.[14] The Algonkin languages also contain many words that seem to have been borrowed from Norse, and one writer, Sherwin, has tabulated seven volumes of what he believes is evidence in this direction.[15] Another situation that might speak for peaceful interaction between the Indian and the Norseman is that of the Beothuk Indians of New-foundland. When modern white men first encountered them they were completely friendly and desirous of trade,[16] and it was not until they were mistreated that they became hostile. Similar situations have been observed among other Indian tribes of the northeastern seaboard.[17] All indications are that the Indians were a friendly people until white man discovered that red man was not mentioned in the Bible and began to invent practices such as scalping.[18] A third group of Indians in the St. Lawrence area, the Iroquois, has a curious past history which anthropologists have been at a loss to explain. One writer, Mallery, has moved to fill the gap of information with a proposal of extensive Norse contact and eventual Iroquois absorption of the Norsemen. He cites cultural influence ranging from the arts, legal practices and architecture to vocabulary loan-words as support for his hypothesis.[19]

In fact, trade with the Indians would have been of even greater value to the Norsemen than trade with the Eskimos. The Indians could supply grain, and their lands could supply timber. If the members of the Eastern Settlement were to do any emigrating, it would have been just as natural for them to do so into Indian lands as it was for those from the Western Settlement to emigrate into Eskimo lands.

While there is good hope through archaeology for eventually deciding the question of Norse presence in the land of the Eskimos, such hope cannot be entertained for proof of their presence in the land of the eastern seaboard Indians. For one thing, the huge influx of post-Columbian white man has trampled and plowed up this land to such an extent that most archaeological traces are surely lost. For another thing, the post-Columbian influx occurred essentially simultaneously with any hypothetical dispersal of the Eastern

Settlement, and traces of the two would be quite difficult to differentiate from one another. This is the problem with such discoveries as the aforementioned dry dock at Follins Pond and the Newport Tower. This ambiguity is likely not only for hard archaeological finds, but for folk tales as well. Another special difficulty in dealing with the archaeology of the eastern seaboard is that one cannot be satisfied to simply differentiate on the basis of time between pre-Columbian Norsemen and post-Columbian Europeans. Throughout history, considerable numbers of sailors have, through various misfortunes, found themselves out of control of their ships and drifting in the open Atlantic. Of those that did not sink, a statistically significant portion must have reached some part of the American seaboard alive. While they had no hope of finding their way back home, they would surely have made the best of their situation and lived out their lives, leaving traces, where they were. Such chance encounters of Norsemen or others with the American seaboard are, of course, of no historical significance. They must be differentiated from encounters that maintained two-way communication and whose communications led, at least conjecturally, to consequences.

So, to entertain any hopes for an archaeological answer to the question of how far south the Norsemen attained, one must expect to have either special luck in dealing with these special difficulties or more advanced techniques of investigation than are now available. Both of these, of course, are quite within the realm of possibility. Meanwhile, one is left only with the circumstantial speculations in Chapter 6 suggesting Norse voyages as far as South America.

An unrelated question, but still part of my attempt to corroborate the maps, might have clearer answers. It is the question of how far into the interior of the continent the

Norsemen might have penetrated. That is, what might be *behind* the recurring map of the Quebec/Labrador Peninsula? In the interior there is no danger of archaeological contamination by castaways. Furthermore, the post-Columbian European settlement of the interior did not occur until long after Norse times, so that any early European archaeological finds in the interior should be clear proof of Norse presence.

Actually, the idea of the Norsemen penetrating the interior of the continent need not shock one as completely unprecedented. It has recently been proven that during the early middle ages Scandinavians had become adept at crossing the *Asian* continent via Russian rivers, and according to pre-New World geographical theory (the Grand Misunderstanding), that is exactly what they would now be doing—exploring the interior of Asia. In their own minds, they would at most have been rediscovering something their ancestors had already known; however, by first traveling west instead of east.

As it turns out, a very large number of discoveries have been made in the Great Lakes area which have been clearly indicative archaeologically of Norse civilization. Not unexpectedly, critics have bitterly attacked their authenticity, sometimes with good reason. The most spectacular of these discoveries is the rune stone found near the town, on the endpaper map, of Kensington, Minnesota. The controversial inscription on the Kensington rune stone describes an overwhelming attack on the Norse explorers by Indians. If this inscription were genuine, it would suggest that the natives of the interior were not always as welcoming of strangers as I have indicated the eastern seaboard Indians were. Indeed, it is known historically that certain tribes were war-like irrespective of later white man's mis-dealings. But if some

enthusiasts are right, the Kensington encounter might have
been the exception rather than the rule. Several writers believe that a genetic remnant of the Norsemen was to be
found in the Mandan Indians of central North Dakota. Before their extinction by a smallpox epidemic in the middle
1800s, the Mandans were described by many visitors as
having an obvious mixture of Caucasian blood, and many
writers have discerned European influences in their folk-
lore.[20] That these cross-racial and cross-cultural ties arose
during extensive contacts with Norsemen is the easiest explanation. Several writers believe this explanation to be
corroborated by the so-called Verendrye stone. This inscribed stone was discovered by the French explorer La
Vérendrye in 1738 during the first organized modern exploration into the Mandan area.[21] Its inscribed characters
were unfamiliar to the original French scholars who studied
it, but they described the characters in such a way that
more recent scholars have concluded they might have been
Nordic runes.[22] The stone was sent back to Paris for further
study, but was evidently lost. Such are the frustrations of
history, for no known copy of the inscription was ever made.

A more tangible discovery is the so-called Beardmore find
near the endpaper's Lake Nipigon in Ontario. Here in the
early 1930s an amateur gold prospector exploring the bottom of a cliff found that the cliff had evidently been selected centuries before as a natural grave monument. He
uncovered a grave containing remains of a Norse sword,
shield and battle-ax.[23] The Beardmore find was subsequently attacked as a fraud, but evidently neither side in
the controversy which ensued can give a convincing argument for its contention.[24] In addition to these finds, early
generations of farmers in the Great Lakes area found while
plowing their fields a collection of apparently Norse arti-

facts which rivals the Indian arrowhead collections of many of their counterparts in other localities.[25] These have been subjected to varying degrees of inconclusive tests in attempts to establish their authenticity.[26] Some, in any case, have been shown to be misunderstood pioneer artifacts.[27]

One writer, Ole Landsverk, has pointed out the interesting fact that many of the not otherwise explained discoveries lie very close to the continental divide which separates the Hudson Bay watershed, on the endpaper map, from the Mississippi River watershed,[28] and he speculates that they were left when Norse explorers could no longer proceed upstream by boat (canoe) from Hudson Bay and had to take to foot.[29] I make the additional observation that most of the discoveries that do not fit this hypothesis do, in fact, lie near the headstreams of the St. Lawrence system, primarily near feeders to the Great Lakes. Lake Nipigon in particular, which feeds into the St. Lawrence system, also lies very close to streams that flow into Hudson Bay. Hjalmar Holand has made several finds along lake shores near these watershed divides. He believes these to be mooring holes cut into large boulders for boats on Norse exploratory expeditions. The implication of this theory of exploration, with one thrust coming upstream from the Hudson Bay area, on the endpaper map, and another upstream from the St. Lawrence, then meeting at the divide, would very neatly explain why the Quebec/Labrador Peninsula appeared as an entity in itself in the European maps.

Thus ends the list of the known or suggested traces of the Greenlanders' dispersal to the north, west, south and the continental interior. So far, one has nothing more to shed light on the extent of the dispersal. Nevertheless, is this information enough to corroborate an assertion that all of the maps I have mentioned are Norse maps? Perhaps not. Indeed, almost certainly many of the earlier maps are Eskimo maps made before the Norsemen learned map making from them. Just as certainly, however, any assertion that they are *all* Eskimo maps has been thoroughly refuted. The Norsemen did indeed disperse into and explore America and did indeed make maps of those explorations just before the European "Age of Discovery." The question of exactly which maps are Norse will require further detailed study elsewhere of the maps themselves.

Finally, one must divert his attention from the extension in space of the Norse people in America and concentrate on their extension in time. The first recorded modern glimpse of the Greenland area since the classical Norse period was provided by the English expeditions under Sir Martin Frobisher in 1576–78, fruitlessly seeking gold in what turned out to be Baffin Island. The members of this expedition seem to have heard rumors about still-living Norsemen. There, on their second voyage, they met some native Eskimos who made "signs of certain people who wear bright plates of gold on their foreheads, and other places of their bodies."[30] How the Englishmen, who had gold fever to begin with, were able to differentiate between gold and copper via sign language is difficult to imagine. It is much easier to imagine them talking themselves into an interpretation of copper as gold, as in the following report:

They [the Eskimos] used to traffic and exchange their commodities with some other people, of whom they have such things, as their miserable country, and ignorance of art to make, denyeth them to have; as bars of iron, heads of iron for their darts, needles made foresquare, certain buttons of copper, which they use to wear upon their foreheads for ornament, as our ladies in the Court of England do use great pearls.

Also they have made signs unto us, that they have seen gold, and such bright plates of metals, which are used for ornaments amongst some people, with whom they have conference.[31]

The only reasonable interpretation of this is that the metal referred to was copper, in light of the existence of copper areas in the central Arctic. The Eskimos never had "conference" with the Indians, and even so, the Indians of their part of the world had no access to or use of either copper or gold. Furthermore, the modern Copper Eskimos themselves have never used the copper in any ornamental way, and this feature sounds more like something introduced or used by Norsemen. The report ties the source of copper together with the source of iron, which also seems to reflect a contemporaneous influence of Norsemen. Along the same line, the Eskimos are never known to have used sails on their boats until they continually contacted white man. Nevertheless, the same report says:

They have one sort of greater boat [umiak], wherein they carry twenty persons and have a mast with a sail thereon, which sail is made of thin skins or bladders, sewed together with the sinews of fishes.[32]

Of course, it is possible to explain many such phenomena on the basis of unrecorded contacts with other Europeans in the eighty years that had elapsed since the post-Columbian discovery of the continent, and undoubtedly many fishermen from Newfoundland and pirates did visit these parts without leaving records. However, the description given of the Eskimos' commerce does not have the flavor one would expect to find if such commerce were at rare intervals with strange peoples instead of ongoing with familiar neighbors. The last of Frobisher's three voyages did not go directly to Baffin Island, but first came around the southern tip of Greenland and entered an ice-free fiord,[33] which must have been near the old Eastern Settlement. There the crew found an Eskimo settlement, from which the inhabitants fled upon their approach. It contained not only the usual Eskimo artifacts but, according to the official record keeper of the voyage, "nails like scupper nails and a trivet of iron."[34] A captain of one of the ships reported that they saw "a box of small nails . . . with diverse other things artificially wrought."[35] These presumed Inugsuk Eskimos would have had little use for such items as an iron trivet in their original form, and Stefansson takes the fact that they were not yet beaten into harpoon heads or needles as evidence of recent European contact with the area of the Eastern Settlement.[36] Indeed, the fact that the Eskimos ran away when the Englishmen approached suggests that they had recently been frightened by the kind of greeting Europeans were infamous for in the New World.

The situation was entirely different when John Davis visited the neighborhood of the old Western Settlement in 1585-87. It is quite unlikely that any previous unrecorded voyages went this far up the coast, and here Davis found the Eskimos apparently so used to friendly interaction with white man—Norsemen still living—that the Eskimos themselves initiated overtures to trade.[37] One of them was even familiar with the thoroughly European custom of kissing the hand.[38] There Davis' party apparently saw one of the Inugsuk coopered tubs,[39] and a grave with a cross over it.[40] (This statement of interpretation of what was seen must be taken skeptically, however. If it had been clearly a Christian cross, one would expect far more comment from the discoverers than was actually made. In particular, Davis' group had no knowledge of the Norse activities and should have thought all the inhabitants heathen.) The Eskimos immediately displayed that they had somewhere learned a deep-rooted appreciation for the use of iron and began thieving whatever iron-containing items they could from the Englishmen. They stole a complete anchor[41] and disassembled a temporarily unattended boat for its nails.[42] They also had their own supply of copper and even copper ore.[43] This ore would have been completely useless to the Eskimos without some contact with living Norsemen, who knew how to smelt ore.

Nearly a century later in 1656 one Nicholas Tunes visited the latitude of the Western Settlement* and said:

As to the people who inhabit this land, our travellers saw two kinds, who live together in good accord and perfect amity. The one are of tall stature, well built physically, of a rather fair complection and very swift of foot. The others are very much smaller, of olive complection, their members fairly well proportioned except that their legs are short and thick. The first take delight in hunting, to which they are inclined by reason of their agility and their natural aptness; the others occupy themselves with fishing. Both of them have very white and close set teeth, black hair, bright eyes, and features so regular that no deformity is to be remarked.[44]

If the first kind of people were actually surviving Norsemen rather than surviving castaways of a later era, one need postulate only a moderate amount of non-preferential intermarriage to see that their blond hair yielded to the black hair of the Eskimos.

Some twenty years after Tunes's experience, a French adventurer La Hontan found himself in a different part of the New World, at the watershed divide between the head of

---

* The historical record only preserves the latitude and no explicit statement of which side of Davis Strait they were on.

the Missouri River and the Red River (of the north) which feeds Hudson Bay. There in 1688 La Hontan met an Indian who wore "a reddish sort of copper medal hanging upon his neck," evidently similar to those described by the Eskimos Frobisher found a century earlier. When asked of the source of this medal, the Indian gave travel directions which seemed to point to Hudson Bay and described a people he called the *Tahuglauk*, a rather Eskimo sounding name. However, the Indian, La Hontan reports, "assured me on the faith of a savage that the Tahuglauk wear their beards two finger breadths long."[45]

All these observations speak rather strongly for an ongoing interdependent relationship between the Eskimos and the Norsemen, and a development of Inugsuk culture to a high level of relative sophistication, especially in the use of metals. When one is faced with such an interdependent situation, it is quite natural to raise the question of what would happen to the system if one of the parties were removed.[46] What would have happened to the Inugsuk culture if the Norsemen had disappeared? Would that culture then have degenerated? The answer to this leading question is contained in all the archaeological reports of investigations of the descendants of the Thule/Inugsuk culture, the post-historic or modern, primitive Eskimo cultures. And all writers on this subject describe the historic Eskimo cultures as degenerated and nebulous in comparison with the Thule and Inugsuk. (Even more spectacular would be the collapse of the contemporary non-primitive Eskimo culture if modern white man were to disappear.[47]) The general disappearance of the Thule/Inugsuk culture evidently did coincide in time with the eventual disappearance of the Norsemen.

When Hans Egede arrived in Greenland in 1721 with a specific desire to seek out remnants of the original Norse colonists, he found no living traces of them either in the Western Settlement or the Eastern Settlement, even though he spent much of his life looking. (Egede was confused about the actual location of the two settlements, but without realizing it visited the ruins of both several times.) Since then, uninformed conjectures about the cause of the disappearance of the Norsemen have varied from Eskimo wars to the Black Death, agricultural pests, abandonment by the European world, starvation through various agencies, racial degeneration, etc.[48] But Ingstad has shown each of these conjectures for one reason or another[49] to be inadequate in explaining the *complete* disappearance of the race. I think that at least the Eastern Settlement lost many inhabitants through the agency suggested by Nansen, Stefansson and Ingstad—piracy. As the early Renaissance gave way to more sinister eras and slavery again came to be fashionable, there was just as much demand for blond-haired slaves as black-faced ones. The only important qualifications of a potential slave beyond strength were that he be a non-Christian and have no strong national government to protect him. The many claims that the Greenlanders had drifted away from Christianity into heathendom may have given many a pirate courage to capture and sell them, and the population of the Eastern Settlement could soon have been consumed.

This process would have had no direct effect, however, on the dispersed people from the Western Settlement or any such from the Eastern. In accounting for the disappearance of these dispersed Norsemen, one must attempt to find out whether or not the simultaneous disappearance of the Thule/Inugsuk culture and the Norsemen is more than coincidental. Central to the question is, of course, the degree of interdependence and the degree of separateness that existed between the two cultures. The acquisition of this knowledge, naturally, will come only after much further field work and excavation. If only as a stimulus for further comment, I can conceive of three theoretically plausible outcomes: 1) that because the Norsemen had to share sea-mammal hunting with the Eskimos to supplement an unhealthy all-caribou diet, when changes of whale populations caused difficulties for the Eskimos the Norsemen could no longer be sustained; or 2) that the Norsemen continued westward, eventually passing into the real Asia and ultimately back to Scandinavia; or 3) that the Norsemen became absorbed into the Eskimo race somewhere in the central Arctic and into the Indian race somewhere in the Great Lakes neighborhood.

The latter seems to me the more likely. In any case, the settlements themselves probably had no more European visitors, even pirates, after the 1500s. From that time on, all European interest in the Western Hemisphere was directed farther south, and from then on dispersal into hunting grounds of anyone remaining in the settlements would have been inevitable. And in a dispersed state they could not possibly hope to maintain their Norse identity. They became simply Americans.

But the European movement to America which they had started has lived on. They deserve credit for it.

Epilogue

By Thor Heyerdahl

With his book *Viking America* James Robert Enterline has opened the door to unexplored chambers in world history. With a new and unexpected approach, instead of hammering at the long bolted gate, he has entered an open window and unlocked the door from within. He did not fumble his way blindly, but followed well-known maps which he wisely read with the eyes of their pre-Columbian creators. He simply bore in mind that these maps were drawn after the time of Leif Eiriksson and before the time of Christopher Columbus. Expressed in other terms: during the very five centuries when the Kingdom of Norway was subordinated to the Roman Catholic Church, i.e., after the tenth-century abolishment of the heathen faith and prior to the sixteenth-century introduction of Protestantism. The maps restudied by Enterline were thus created by medieval geographers at a time when the Christian Norse colony on Greenland kept its Catholic sovereign in Norway fully informed of its own explorations involving Vinland. And yet, before either the Norsemen themselves or the world geographers realized that from Greenland and Vinland, a large continent unexplored by Europeans extended southward to split the vast world ocean into two parts: the Atlantic and the Pacific.

The impact in Enterline's argumentation lies precisely in his observation that the medieval concept of the Arctic region was different from the actual one known to us today: To them, it was not an open sea but some sort of serpentine Polar coast with rocky peninsulas emerging from eternal ice, extending from the Norse kingdoms in Scandinavia and westward to Greenland and as far as Norse settlements extended.

The reader who has followed Enterline's guided tour inside *Viking America,* does well in leaning back for a while digesting the novel food for thought until the new horizons stand out clearly. Old questions emerge as new. Who did, and who did not, discover America?

Did Columbus discover the New World as the textbooks say? He certainly did if we are willing to admit that there were also people ashore on the other side who discovered Columbus when he landed. The meeting of two great worlds was indeed the achievement of Columbus, and Columbus alone. He changed history, both in the Old World and in the New, and history is forever there to prove it. But did not the Vikings get ashore in the New World centuries before the Spaniards? Yes they did, and the written sagas are now also conclusively confirmed by modern archaeologists with on-the-spot excavations and carbon datings in Newfoundland. Were the Viking ships and the Spanish caravels the first vessels to explore the American coasts? No indeed, they were not. The *Vikings* recorded that they had both traded and fought with local people they termed *"Skraellings,"* who sailed the Davis Strait between America and Greenland in boats of skin. The *Spaniards* recorded that they both traded and fought with local people they termed *"Indians,"* who sailed the sea on both sides of the Panama Isthmus, some in canoes, some in large reed ships, and others on balsa rafts carrying up to twenty tons of precious merchandise. These local sailors, too, had their own legitimate claim as to who had discovered their own country. They, in turn, claimed that some of their ancestors had come across the Atlantic like the Spaniards, under the leadership of a priest-king referred to in Mexico as Quetzalcoatl. He differed from the primitive tribes of beardless redskins who received him in having a white complexion and long beard, while wearing a girdled gown, sandals, and carrying a staff. From these features some of the Spaniards mistook the venerated discoverer for a wandering Apostle from the Holy Land. The Mexican scribes had recorded his arrival with hieroglyphics in real books, and the local artists had painted him on paper and ceramics, or chiseled him in enduring rock ever since the days when he was supposed to have landed. Quetzalcoatl and his bearded crew were said to have brought civilization to the barbarous food gatherers who were there to receive them: They were said to have brought with them across the Atlantic everything from the art of writing and medicine to pyramid building and cotton cultivation.

Who was this Semitic-looking culture-hero recalled and depicted among the beardless Indians? And, before his alledged arrival by sea, who had found the way to America for the illiterate original jungle dwellers who, according to the Mexicans themselves, were already there to receive Quetzalcoatl?

Nobody knows. The name, the birthplace and year of arrival of the first illiterate stone-age discoverer of America will never be known. Whoever he was, this roving family father could hardly have realized that he himself, at a given moment, had set foot on a new continent, until then purely an animal kingdom. However, all evidence indicates that these first migrant ancestors of the Skraellings entered the American side of the icy Behring Strait from Asia at least fifteen or twenty thousand years before the first Viking ship was launched into the North Sea. Future archaeology may push this human discovery of America back to even more remote ages.

The pedigree of the subsequently arriving Quetzalcoatl also remains unidentified. Future archaeology may perhaps disclose that his traveling party was one of the countless groups of sunworshipping explorers, traders and colonists that voyaged in primitive craft between islands and coasts of the Mediterranean world since the local birth of civilization. Although, to our knowledge, the main waves of organized Phoenician colonization outside Gibraltar began to occupy the unsheltered Atlantic coasts of Africa and Spain about 1200 B.C., much earlier voyages of major impact had begun to spread westward across the entire Mediterranean about 3000 B.C. After several hundred thousand years of obscure prehistory, civilization was born just about simultaneously in Mesopotamia, coastal Syria and Palestine, Egypt, Cyprus, and Crete, all about 3000 B.C. Is it a mere coincidence that the Maya Indians, on the other side of the Atlantic, also begin their own very exact calendar then? The Maya calendar begins with a date convertible in our calendar to August 12, 3113 B.C. Why this choice of a zero year? Did Quetzalcoatl reach America then, or did something of paramount importance happen then in the former oversea abode of those who devised the Maya calendar? Future research may perhaps disclose this secret.

Who, then, discovered America?

A forever-forgotten Asiatic hunter—for the Skraellings. The still unidentified sun-priest Quetzalcoatl—for the Olmecs,

Toltecs and Aztecs. The Christian Greenland colonist Leif Eiriksson—for the Norsemen. But Columbus for the world.

Columbus' own Italian shore, Liguria, has by choice become the home of the present writer, though brought up in Norway with the Norse sagas in their original texts. Yet he chose to cross the sea in wash-through rafts of stout timber or flexible reeds: water-craft available on both sides of the ocean in the days of Quetzalcoatl and the Skraellings. In addition to having practical experience of some of the maritime problems involved, the writer therefore also feels disinvolved in patriotic prestige, which sometimes shrouds a fair approach to studies of the earliest voyages to America. It can hardly be ignored, however, that overseas discoveries can be classed in two separate categories: those that result from accidental drift caused by mishap or faulty navigation, and those that are premeditated and result from brainwork and meticulous planning.

It is evident that Columbus' discovery was not the result of accidental drift. Any reader of his personal log will be convinced of his determined search for something he expected to find through deliberate calculations and planning. There are those who, for fear of depriving this great pioneer of the fullest honor for his discovery, inadvertently strive to reduce him to a mere bold navigator who accidentally happened to hit upon America just because America was there to block his way. This is an unfair image of a man who, in addition to being bold and brave, also had imaginative vision, intelligence and a perfectly sound, scholarly approach to the problem he was determined to tackle. Those who want to reduce Columbus to a mere adventurous tar do him a poor service indeed. If, as they infer, his advanced calculations were restricted to a notion that the earth was round, then he must have made a completely erroneous estimate of its circumference and by sheer coincidence stumbled upon America the very day he had figured out he should have reached Asia. Columbus had not even sailed one quarter of the distance to Asia, and only one fifth of the distance to his alleged destination, India, when he reached land precisely where he had said he would find it. To the bewilderment of everybody, including himself, it was not India but a new world. When Magellan later rounded this unexplored continent, he still had to cross another ocean, which alone spanned exactly half the circumference of the world, before he reached the coveted spice islands in front of Asia.

Indeed, Columbus' masterly planned expedition deserves more credit than luck and courage. He reached the coast he was aiming for according to his preconceived plan, precisely as he himself had expected and predicted. And this is where Enterline, by approaching existing medieval maps with a medieval map-reader's mind, unveils Columbus as a meticulous, intellectual organizer with sound and correct calculations rather than as a daredevil who barely escaped disaster because America happened to be there when his crew had reached the limit of exhaustion and yet, theoretically, should have had four times further to go.

True, Columbus was convinced that the earth was round, and this gave him his controversial sailing direction, but not his preconceived sailing distance. As Enterline shows, although religious teachings in the fifteenth century still tried to preserve the concept of a flat earth, its spherical form had been recognized since the time of the early Greek astronomers, who also came amazingly close to an exact calculation of its diameter, about 24,000 miles. These classical Greek results were well known to scholars of Columbus' time. A clue of no mean importance to the understanding of Columbus' preconceived world picture lies indeed in the very fact that he accepted Ptolemy's view of a round earth, yet he rejected Ptolemy's astronomical calculations as to its correct circumference. For reasons not given, Columbus, in preparing his voyage, insisted that the earth was much smaller than figured out by the Greek astronomers, and that the distance to India toward the west was, therefore, only a fraction of what it would have been according to Ptolemaic teachings. However, Columbus had no astronomical means of measuring the circumference of the earth, and his reasoning had therefore obviously followed the opposite direction: Somehow he felt sure he knew the distance to land on the other side of the Atlantic, which he thought must be India, and on the basis of this distance he came to his conclusion that the earth must be much smaller than assumed by the Greeks. Columbus, in fact, died in the belief that it was India he had reached, and that it was exactly as close to Europe as he had said in advance. Since he knew that the distance to India had been farther for those who had sailed in the opposite direction, and perhaps because he began to ponder about the vast discrepancies between his own and the Greek calculations, he came to a very remarkable conclusion on the earth's shape after his third voyage to America: "I find that it is not as round as it is described, but it is shaped like a pear, which is round everywhere except near the stalk where it projects strongly; or it is like a very round ball with something like a woman's nipple in one place, and this projecting part is highest and the one nearest heaven."

Columbus has been scorned for this seemingly absurd distortion of the spheric Ptolemaic world, but once again for no fair reason. In fact, his conclusion was quite meaningful, even logical, when we bear in mind that his trans-Atlantic voyage at that time was supposed to have reached distant Asia, as no one had yet crossed the Panama Isthmus or circumnavigated Tierra del Fuego to detect the confusion. Thus, assumably, Columbus had come all the way to the remote spice islands east of India by sailing a shorter way across the "upper" northern hemisphere than was otherwise needed to reach these far islands for those who had visited them by way of the "lower" southern hemisphere. Hence, Columbus concluded, the earth could not be round as he had previously assumed, but pear-shaped, with the pointed end up. His reasoning was anything but stupid.

Enterline has shown why Columbus was so sure of having reached India, and why he succeeded in landing according to his own exact plan. He had drawn his own conclusions from the geographical knowledge available to any inquisitive mind in Europe at his time: the existence of land on the opposite side of the North Atlantic. Greenland had for more than four centuries been an inhabited Christian colony, and many contemporary geographers suspected that it might be the most northerly extension of eastern Asia. Eastern Asia was already explored by Columbus' compatriot, Marco Polo. The Norse colonists on Greenland, during their repeated unsuccessful attempts to settle among warlike and numerically superior Skraellings in Vinland, must have perceived enough of the coastline further south to reach their own controversial impression that Vinland extended southward into Africa, a belief repeated in several of their medieval texts. Since early Viking times the maritime Norwegians had been well familiar with the northern section of Africa, distinguishing between the Arab domain along the Mediterranean coast (*Store Serkland* or Great Tunicland) and the dark continent extending beyond (*Store Blaaland* or Great Negroland). Their voyages into the Mediterranean both westward by way of Russian rivers and the Black Sea, and eastward by way of the British Channel and the open Atlantic, were so common that, when the Catholic Norwegian King Sigurd, in the twelfth century, sailed with "sixty Viking ships splendidly built after the will of God" on a pilgrimage to the Holy Land, he encountered another large Viking fleet in the Strait of Gibraltar, which he had to fight to proceed with his own ships on his sacred mission. Yet the Norsemen were apparently unaware of the fact that below Gibraltar the west coast of Africa dropped sharply off to the south. Columbus, however, as a young man, had been down the west coast of Africa as far as Guinea, and thus knew that the Norsemen were necessarily wrong in their assumption that Vinland ran into Africa, since Africa, south of Guinea, turned precisely in the opposite direction. With Africa ruled out and tropic America still being an unknown concept, Columbus, prior to his first voyage, could only draw the logical conclusion that Asia with India and its eastward extending islands represented the warm land extending southward from the sub-Arctic Norse colonies in the extreme northwest corner of the world ocean, the only ocean then known to exist.

How much could Columbus, born and raised on the Mediterranean shores, have heard about the lands visited by Norse expeditions in arctic and subarctic regions? The existence and whereabouts of these northern lands were no secrets to Columbus' contemporaries in the Catholic world. The fact that Vinland had been found west of Greenland was already recorded in the *Geography of the Northern Lands* by Adam von Bremen as early as in 1070, more than four centuries prior to Columbus' first voyage. Also, detailed written description with exact sailing directions and geographical specification of Vinland's location to the southwest of Greenland were available among the Christian population on Iceland generations before Columbus' time. Even if Columbus himself did not visit Iceland in 1477, as many assume, he would have got the necessary information from any other sailor who had been there, since most Icelanders knew their written sagas by heart. Christian Norse captives from Greenland well familiar with Vinland either through tradition or direct personal experience, had also been brought in large numbers to England by the active British slave raiders, and it is well known that Columbus personally did visit England. In addition, during his preparations he also corresponded with learned Englishmen well familiar with these publicly criticized trans-Atlantic slave raids. In fact, the English raids on the unprotected Norse settlements along the west coast of Greenland were so well known that a treaty on the subject was reached between the Norwegian and the English kings in 1432, and subsequently Pope Nicholas V stated in writing that the greater number of these Christian slaves had returned from their captivity to Greenland, "and there repaired the ruins of their dwellings . . ." What we should not forget is that the Bristol pirates themselves must have been thoroughly familiar with the lands along the Davis Strait, since they were able to raid the widely separated Norse settlements located along a rugged coast facing America at a couple of hundred miles distance directly on the other side of the Straits. Those who have studied Columbus' life agree that he lost no opportunity to learn during his travels along the Arab coast of Africa to the British Isles and to the Portuguese- and Spanish-owned islands in the Atlantic. He was able to collect tales and traditions and odd facts from sailors and merchants, observations of prevailing trade winds and ocean currents and of the diversified jetsam, boats and bodies thrown up on the beaches of the Canary Islands and the Azores—information that served to support the theory which led to his first voyage into the unknown Atlantic.

Let us ignore for a moment the fact that Columbus trav-

eled wide and far with an open mind for many years before
he became convinced of the exact whereabouts of the land
he was to pinpoint on the other side of the Atlantic. Indeed,
he needed no more to encounter any Norsemen to hear about
Vinland than he needed to go to Greece or Alexandria to
hear the theory that the earth was round. All the knowledge
essential for Columbus to reach the basic conclusion for his
voyage was available in his own Mediterranean peninsula.
What any nation in the Christian world came to learn of
scientific or economic value was quickly known in Rome.
The Norsemen never kept their settlements on Greenland
and explorations of Vinland a secret, but immediately passed
all important information on to the Church in Rome. The
direct ties by land and sea between distant Norway and the
Italian peninsula were stronger than was generally realized.
How many have given a thought to the fact that, none less
than Leif Eiriksson, Vinland's discoverer brought with him
a Catholic priest and Christian teachers when in A.D. 999 he
sailed back from Norway to his father's, Eirik the Red's,
heathen colony on Greenland? Leif Eiriksson brought the
priest on express order from the King or Norway, Holy Olav,
whose relations with Rome were so excellent that he later
became canonized by the Pope, as Saint Olav. His service
to the medieval Church in Rome was precisely that he extended the dominance of this Church from Norway itself to
all the far-flung Norwegian colonies westward across the
North Sea and even across the North Atlantic.

The Catholic priests living with the Norwegian colonies on
Greenland since A.D. 999 were followed by the first bishop
in 1112. By then the Church was so well aware of the existence of new land discovered west of Greenland that the Icelandic annals record that Bishop Eirik Gnupsson, upon his
visit to the Greenland parish, sailed on from there expressly

to visit Vinland. Further details of his activities on the other side of the Atlantic are not preserved, but shortly after the by then Catholic Norse colony on Greenland sent shiploads of walrus tusks, furs and a live polar bear to King Sigurd of Norway, with a request for a permanent bishop on Greenland. This king, who had personally led a Norwegian expedition to Jerusalem—fighting for the Christian cause and thus became known as Sigurd Jordsalfarer (Sigurd Pilgrim-to-the-Holy-Land)—immediately granted the request, and from 1126 the Greenland colony had their own resident bishop. Not long after they had two, since the Norse farms and churches on west Greenland were spread over vast distances.

It is necessary to realize that in the centuries from Leif Eiriksson to Christopher Columbus there was no isolation between the powerful kingdom of Norway and the Mediterranean world. At least four Norwegian kings did personally sail into the Mediterranean with their fleets for the purpose of having a holy bath in the river Jordan. Their moral merits may be doubted, but their fidelity to the Roman Church is well documented. Even their remote Greenland colony was forced by the King of Norway to pay a regular crusader's tax to the Church, spent in the joint efforts of Christian Europe to reconquer the Holy Land from the Saracens. From the twelfth to the fourteenth century the Catholic Church grew to become a real power on Greenland. In this pre-Columbian period seventeen churches were erected on the west coast facing America across the Davis Straits, and in addition to episcopal residence, a cathedral and about 280 farms there were two monasteries, one for nuns dedicated to St. Benedict and one for monks dedicated to St. Olav and St. Augustin. This is known not only from the written records, but also from the actual ruins still present and studied by

Danish archaeologists. The Norse activities also on the Vinland side of the Davis Strait are now corroborated both by the written Icelandic sagas and the recent excavations of the Ingstad group of professional archaeologists, who found and carbon-dated eleventh-century Norse house foundations with a bog-iron-smithy and a spinning whorl at L'Anse aux Meadows on Newfoundland. Accustomed to refer to all early Norsemen on Greenland as "Vikings," we forget that this is a highly abused use of the word: These people were Christian colonists, whereas *viking* was the old Norse term for a seafaring buccaneer and refers no more to the population as a whole than does "pirate" to all their contemporaries from England.

The isolation of the Norse colonies on Greenland from the rest of the Catholic world on the European side of the Atlantic could not avoid certain problems in keeping up with the current Christian rules. The colony was small and marriage between relatives hard to avoid, especially since a Papal decree forbade matrimonies closer than seven generations apart. The Greenland colony had hardly that many generations behind them in the twelfth century, and envoys from Norway went to Rome to ask Pope Alexander III for a dispensation, since twelve days were needed for the remote arctic island colonists to sail elsewhere in search of Christian wives. The Pope consented to let the Norwegian Archbishop give permission for marriages as close as the fifth generation in special cases. However, the sacraments caused further problems in an arctic area where neither grapes nor grain grew. The Greenland parish, therefore, sent a subsequent request to Rome for permission to substitute beer or fermented crowberry juice for wine and meat or other available food for bread, but Pope Gregorius personally interfered with a letter to the Norwegian Archbishop in 1237 where he

insisted that his Greenland parish should at least maintain
the use of bread in the sacraments. In 1276 Pope John XXI
wrote to the Norwegian Archbishop who tried to be released
from his recently imposed duty of personally collecting the
crusaders' tax from the bishops on Greenland, complaining
of the enormous distance and the fury of the great ocean.
But not until 1279 does Pope Nicolas III allow the Archbishop to send an attorney in his own place on the long and
dangerous voyage. Three years later the attorney was back
and the Archbishop wrote to the Pope that the Greenland
parish was poor except in skins and walrus tusks, which have
scant value as crusaders' tax. The Pope, however, did not
yield on the tax imposed on Greenland, and in a letter of
1282 he insists that this remote Christian colony continue to
pay the crusaders' tax in *naturalia* which the Church must
sell in Norway.

The Catholic Church seems to have grown into the leading land-owner on Greenland prior to the population decline
that led to the complete disappearance of the local colonies
around 1500. Rome followed the Greenland activities as long
as the Christian communities survived, however, and ship-
ments from Greenland were checked, sold and taxed as the
ships arrived in Bergen, Norway. Subsequent lists recorded
independently in the sixteenth century by Archbishop Erik
Valkendorf and the historian Absalon Pedersson Beyer of
Bergen concur with the early sagas in indicating how the
Greenland colony obtained much of their furs and timber by
trading across the Davis Strait. The saga of Torfinn Karlsefni recounts that Torfinn traded with the Skraellings during his stay in Vinland, to obtain "skins of squirrels, sable,
and all kinds of furs." Beyer's list of resources available to
the Norse colony on the other side of the Atlantic includes
items such as sable, marten, deer and vast forests; and among

trade objects on the Archbishop's Greenland list are black bear, beaver, otter, ermine, sable, wolverene and lynx, all of which are North American animals non-existent on Greenland. As shown by Enterline, the Greenlanders were known throughout medieval Europe since they, and nobody else, provided the white gyrfalcons so extremely coveted in hunting and non-existent in Europe.

Rome's concern about the imminent loss of the Greenland colony is reflected in the Pope Nicolas V letter of 1448 to two local bishops, the Germans Marcellus and Matheus who, through fraud, misled the Pope to ordain them bishops of Greenland. The Pope states that a fleet of Barbarians had recently assaulted the Norse settlements on Greenland, destroying all sacred edifices except nine parish churches of difficult access due to steep cliffs, but most of the parish were now back in their harassed settlements "longing to re-establish and extend the divine services."

As late as in 1492, the very year Columbus set sail for America, a Papal letter from Rome refers to the now disappearing parish on Greenland as having mainly subsisted on dried fish and milk.

If anything can be said with confidence about Columbus, it is that he was a keen Catholic, closely connected with the Roman Church and undoubtedly sharing in its missionary ambitions as well as in its geographical knowledge. His faith and his knowledge gave him the courage and conviction with which he set out to realize his historic enterprise. This alone will explain why Columbus kept on with his indefatigable efforts for years to persuade the Council of Genoa and the Royal Houses of Portugal, France, England and Spain to lend an ear to his bold assertion that there was land on the other side of the Atlantic at a specifically given distance which was only a quarter of what had hitherto been calculated by all learned men. His faith and his knowledge permitted Columbus to be so sure of his own claim that he was willing to vouch for it with his life. His salesmanship when he raised a fortune for his controversial enterprise was a jigsaw puzzle composed of bits of geographical facts and logical reasoning. He needed more than charm and empty hands to get from the war-ridden rulers of Spain what they would never have offered a foreign sailor from Genoa who had nothing to offer except the idea that the earth was round. The spheric shape of our planet was a well-known theory that the Catholic Majesties in Spain would long ago have accepted or rejected with their own local advisers, and was not worthy of the high price they conceded to Columbus: three equipped expedition vessels; a hundred-and-twenty-man crew including noblemen, civil servants and soldiers; the cash payment of 2,000.000 *maravedis;* the status as a Spanish noble; the rank of Grand Admiral of the Seas; the power as Viceroy and irremovable Governor of all the islands and firm land he himself and anybody else in the future would discover and conquer in the ocean; and the assurance that all these honors were to be inherited by his first-born son from generation to generation. This tremendous price, listed in Columbus' own speech dictated *"In Nomine Domini Nostri Jhesu Christi"* for presentation to King Ferdinand and Queen Isabella of Spain, shows best of all that the foreigner from Genoa had more to sell than mere eloquence. Columbus' later travel companion, the chronicler Las Casas, stresses that before departure Columbus was so sure of the position of the lands he was heading for as if he had had them "in his own room." Also some of the sailors from the first voyage witnessed that Columbus had assured them beforehand that after sailing only eight hundred Spanish miles they could expect to find land, which they did. Columbus consistently followed the 28th northern parallel, the latitude of Florida, which would have brought him far north of any landfall in India or Indonesia. Yet he was so sure of this course that he bluntly refused to turn southsouthwest as demanded by despairing officers and crew who claimed to have detected indications of land in that direction. As shown by Columbus' own journal, against the brewing threat of mutiny, and by keeping a double log to cheat his own companions to believe they were not so far away from home, he insisted that no other course would bring them to firm land as fast as the one he was making them steer. A brief deviation to avoid open revolt led by his second in command showed Columbus to be right. And on October 11, 1492, when his exhausted crew began to give up all hope, and the coast of Asia was still more than half the world's circumference distant, Columbus declared that land would be discovered the next day. Land was discovered the next day: an island in front of Florida with the myriad of islands and the mainland of the Skraellings blocking further passage close behind.

Columbus found the Skraellings and brought Christianity to them. Nobody can deny that he became the historic father of European America, nor that he will forever remain the one historic person whose discoveries have left the greatest impact on all subsequent generations of man. It is an extra credit to this great expedition organizer that he reached land and saved his crew not by luck and coincidence, but by intelligent investigation, logical deduction, and meticulous planning. Enterline's book, by extending our knowledge of the medieval world of the Norsemen, also helps to improve the obscure picture of Columbus. Instead of a stubborn fanatic of a sea dog exposing his crew to unjustifiable risk, he emerges as a man of considerable wisdom and reason, a methodical navigator who overlooked no evidence available to contemporary scholars and the Church in order to reach his goal according to his preconceived plan. To get a clear perspective of the greatest known sea adventure in history, one must visualize, with Columbus and Enterline, a line plotted across the medieval Terra Incognita from Marco Polo's Asia to Viking America.

THOR HEYERDAHL

Colla Micheri, Italy
March 18, 1972

Notes

The format used to refer to entries in the bibliography is explained by the following example:

Nansen, 1911a, 2, p. 100.

This refers to page 100 of a work published by the author Nansen in the year 1911. Since the bibliography contains several works of Nansen's for 1911, the "a" specifies the first on the list for that year. This happens to be a two-volume work, and the "2" specifies the second volume. Thus, the example refers to page 100 of Volume 2 of Nansen's *In Northern Mists*. A simplified format suffices for most entries.

CHAPTER 1

1. Mulroy, pp. 93–100.
2. Nansen, 1911a, 1, p. 255.
3. Beamish, pp. 173–78.
4. Gordon, 1971.
5. Hallberg, pp. 10–17.
6. *Scandinavia*, 1, pp. 31–44.
7. *Scandinavia*, 1, p. 45.
8. G. Jones, 1968, pp 20–21.
9. *Scandinavia*, 1, p. 67.
10. Piggott, pp. 14–15.
11. ———, p. 257.
12. Simpson, pp. 154–59.
13. Reeves, pp. 161–62, no. 9.
14. see, however, Guthmundsson, 1967.
15. Piggott, pp. 144–45; Hovgaard, pp. 51–68.
16. Simpson, p. 81.
17. Cassidy, pp. 80–83.
18. Diringer, pp. 507–24.
19. *Scandinavia*, 1, pp. 73 ff.
20. Simpson, p. 156.

21. Piggott, p. 16.
22. G. Jones, 1968, pp. 334–45.
23. Hallberg, p. 8.
24. Reeves, p. 160, no. 2.
25. Gathorne-Hardy, 1921, pp. 89–93.
26. T. Andersson, pp. 82–83.
27. Hallberg, pp. 55–56.
28. Hallberg, p. 35.
29. G. Jones, 1968, pp. 315–34.

30. *Scandinavia*, 1, pp. 130–34.
31. Sveinsson, p. 15.
32. Mallery, pp. 43–44, 47.
33. Stefansson, 1942, p. 7.
34. ———, 1942, pp. 8, 288.
35. *Meddelelser om Grönland*, Vols. 67, 76, 88, 89, 90.
36. Fossum, pp. 11–27.
37. Merrill, 1935.
38. T. Andersson, 1964.

CHAPTER 2

1. Ingstad, 1969; Collins, 1970.
2. Ingstad, 1969, p. 221.
3. Beamish, pp. 179–232.
4. Ingstad, 1969, p. 197.
5. ———, 1969, p. 203.
6. Sauer, p. 183; Kaups, 1971.
7. Ingstad, 1969, pp. 219–21.
8. Hermansson, 1944, p. 50; G. Jones, 1964, pp. 148–49.
9. Hermansson, 1944, p. 49; G. Jones, 1964, p. 147.
10. Stefansson, 1938, 1, p. 95.
11. U.S.A.F. Operational Navigation Chart C-12, D-15.
12. Hermansson, 1944, p. 22; G. Jones, 1964, pp. 178–79.
13. ———, 1964, p. 147.
14. ———, 1964, p. 172.
15. Roussell, 1941, pp. 19–27.
16. ———, 1936, p. 43.
17. Tikhomirov, pp. 24–30.
18. Soper, p. 113, 115.
19. McGill, p. 45.
20. Roussell, 1941, p. 20.
21. Flaherty, p. 120.

22. e.g., G. Jones, 1964, p. 179.
23. Hermansson, 1944, p. 22.
24. ———, 1944, pp. 57–58; G. Jones, 1964, p. 158.
25. Roussell, 1936, pp. 103–5.
26. Hermansson, 1944, p. 53; G. Jones, 1964, p. 152.
27. Hermansson, 1944, pp. 27–28; G. Jones, 1964, p. 184.
28. Maycock, 1963.
29. Lamb, pp. 64–65.
30. Weeks, p. 89.
31. Reman, p. 185.
32. Polunin, 1, pp. 157–58.
33. ———, pp. 167–70.
34. ———, pp. 171–72.
35. Reeves, p. xvii.
36. Gray, p. 99; Sauer, p. 125.
37. Reeves, p. 170 no. 36.
38. Gray, p. 160.
39. Reeves, p. 161 no. 6.
40. G. Jones, 1964, p. 149.
41. Hermansson, 1944, p. 50; G. Jones, 1964, p. 149.
42. ———, 1964, p. 90.
43. Ingstad, 1966, p. 154.

CHAPTER 3

1. H. Jones, 1964.
2. Nansen, 1911a, 2, pp. 63–64.
3. ———, 1911a, 2, p. 4 n. 1.
4. Ingstad, 1966, p. 70.
5. G. Jones, 1964, pp. 181–82.
6. ———, 1964, p. 189.
7. ———, 1964, p. 172.
8. Hovgaard, pp. 147–52.
9. Ingstad, 1966, pp. 150–51.
10. Nansen, 1911a, 1, p. 190.
11. ———, 1911a, 1, p. 257.
12. ———, 1911a, 1, p. 268 n. 2.
13. G. Jones, 1964, p. 180.
14. ———, 1964, pp. 150–51.
15. Reman, pp. 86–88;
    Hovgaard, p. 159;
    Pohl, 1966, pp. 105–6.
16. Ingstad, 1966, p. 204;
    Pohl, 1966, pp. 175–76.

17. Nansen, 1911a, 1, p. 343.
18. ———, 1911a, 1, p. 343.
19. M. Jones, p. 8.
20. ———, p. 15.
21. Polunin, 1, pp. 287–95;
    Porsild, 1957, pp. 117–24, 190–92.
22. M. Jones, p. 57.
23. Durand, p. 443.
24. Sveinsson, pp. 9–10.
25. Polunin, 1, p. 292 n. 2.
26. Hermansson, 1936.
27. Reeves, p. 164 no. 13.
28. Ingstad, 1966, p. 138.
29. ———, 1966, p. 138.
30. Stefansson, 1940, pp. 43–47.
31. Nansen, 1911a, 1, pp. 358 ff.
32. ———, 1911b, pp. 579–80.
33. Ingstad, 1966, p. 150.

CHAPTER 4

1. Kaups, 1970.
2. Reman, p. 59.
3. Canadian Hydrographic Service, p. 239.
4. Grenfell, p. 68.
5. Polunin, 3, p. 203.
6. Tanner, 1, p. 351.
7. Drinnan and Prior, p. 31.
8. Nowosad, p. 15.
9. Flaherty, pp. 131, 132.
10. Nowosad, p. 15.
11. Stefansson, 1940, pp. 286–360.
12. Reman, pp. 140–64.
13. Adam, 1959, p. 32;
    ———, 1967.
14. Tanner, 1, p. 308.
15. *Arctic Pilot*, 3, pp. 235–36.
16. Beamish, pp. 64–65, 234–39.
17. Torfaeus, 1891, pp. 75–79.
18. *Arctic Pilot*, 3, p. 219.

19. *Labrador and Hudson Bay Pilot*, p. 288.
20. Grenfell, p. 102.
21. *Labrador and Hudson Bay Pilot*, p. 283.
22. Hovgaard, p. 235.
23. *Canadian Weekly Bulletin*, Nov. 13, 1968, p. 6.
24. Tanner, 1, pp. 308–9.
25. Tanner, 1, p. 373.
26. *Arctic Pilot*, 3, pp. 232–33.
27. Polunin, 3, pp. 203–4.
28. Reman, pp. 190–91.
29. Krogh, pp. 20–37.
30. Lee, 1968b;
    ———, 1969.
31. ———, 1968a, p. 20.
32. ———, 1969. p. 30.
33. ———, 1969, p. 72.
34. Bird, 1969.

CHAPTER 5

1. Morison, 1965.
2. Nansen, 1911a, 1, pp. 185–86.
3. W. Taylor, 1959.
4. Ingstad, 1966, p. 313 ff.
5. Mathiassen, 1927, 2, p. 1.
6. ———, 1927, 2, p. 184.
7. Bagrow, pp. 26–27;
   Cooper, 1971.
8. Boas, pp. 235–39;
   Rasmussen, 1931, pp. 91–113.
9. Stefansson, 1942, pp. 201–2.
10. Washburn, 1962.
11. Nansen, 1911a, 1, p. 13.
12. Lattimore, p. 64;
    Nansen, 1911a, 1, p. 114.
13. ———, 1911a, 2, p. 239.
14. ———, 1911a, 2, p. 271.
15. Thomson, pp. 382–83.

16. Beazley, 1, pp. 328–32;
    Cassidy, Chaps. 2–7.
17. Brown, pp. 88–90.
18. Thomson, pp. 389–90.
19. Ingstad, 1966, p. 317.
20. Stefansson, 1942, pp. 205–7.
21. Wood and Fyfe, pp. 509–10.
22. Stefansson, 1939, Chap. 1.
23. Arctic Pilot, 3, pp. 47–58.
24. Neatby, 1958, pp. 52–55, 84–91.
25. Ingstad, 1966, p. 329–30.
26. ———, 1966, p. 330.
27. Stefansson, 1938, 2, pp. 240–41;
    Neatby, 1966, p. 87.
28. S. Larsen, pp. 65–66.
29. Carus-Wilson, pp. 71–157.
30. Nörlund, p. 182.

CHAPTER 6

1. Holborn, 1968.
2. Morison, 1971, p. 101.
3. Stover, Chap. 3.
4. Donworth, p. 111.
5. De Costa, 1872, p. 21.
6. Haugen, pp. 160–69.
7. Cassidy, p. 169.
8. Foucault, pp. xi, 221.
9. Goldstein, 1965, pp. 12–13.
10. Morison, 1942, pp. 65–68.
11. Donworth, pp. 120–31.

12. ———, pp. 175–78.
13. Stefansson, 1940, pp. 109–11.
14. Tornöe, 1967, pp. 94–102.
15. Quinn, 1961, p. 284.
16. Nunn, pp. 31–53.
17. Wise, pp. 290–98.
18. Las Casas, p. 104.
19. De Costa, 1872, pp. 22–23.
20. Beazley, 2, pp. 3, 17–19, 105.
21. Piggott, pp. 82–91.
22. Parry, p. 3.

CHAPTER 7

1. Mathiassen, 1931, p. 284 ff.
2. Holtved, 1944.
3. Harp, p. 125.
4. W. Taylor, 1959, pp. 38–39.
5. Mathiassen, 1936.
6. Vebaek, p. 736.
7. Wolfe, p. 388.

8. Nares, 1, p. 88;
   ———, 2, p. 162.
9. Moss, pp. 21–22.
10. G. Isachsen, 1907.
11. Lee, 1968b, p. 146.
12. Ingstad, 1966, pp. 95–96.
13. Simmons, pp. 190–91.

14. Oleson, p. 41;
    G. Isachsen, 1904.
15. Isachsen and Isachsen, p. 78.

16. Ingstad, 1969, p. 140.
17. Reeves, p. xx.
18. Mathiassen, 1927, 1, p. 193.

CHAPTER 8

1. *Scandinavia*, 1, p. 125.
2. Lamb, pp. 65–66;
   Nörlund, pp. 237–44;
   Dansgaard, 1969;
   Ladurie, 1971, Chap. 6.
3. *Conference on Climate*, pp. 31–32.
4. Degerböl, 1936, p. 3.
5. ———, 1934, p. 150.
6. Kelsall, p. 125.
7. ———, pp. 143–46.
8. ———, pp. 211–12.
9. ———, p. 216.
10. Oleson, pp. 65–66.
11. O'Neill, pp. 53–73.
12. Stefansson, 1929, p. 294.
13. Quimby, 1962.
14. Jenness, 1922, p. 29.
15. Small, 1968.
16. Fischer-Møller, 1942, p. 76.
17. Stefansson, 1942, pp. 170–76.
18. ———, 1929, pp. 192–93.
19. Jenness, 1923, pp. 46–47.
20. ———, 1923, p. 44.
21. Sullivan, pp. 225–28.
22. Noice, pp. 228–32.
23. Levin, pp.212–28.

24. Cavalli-Sforza, p. 37.
25. Stefansson, 1914, p. vi.
26. Rasmussen, 1931, p. 113.
27. Mathiassen, 1928.
28. Kelsall, pp. 213–16.
29. Fischer-Möller, 1937, pp. 62–63.
30. Meldgaard, pp. 176–77.
31. Harp, p. 170.
32. Rasmussen, 1931, p. 115.
33. Harp, p. 114.
34. Rasmussen, 1931, p. 115.
35. Neatby, 1966.
36. Rasmussen, 1931, p. 114.
37. Jenness, 1922, pp. 57–58.
38. Stefansson, 1914, pp. 297, 298.
39. Oleson, p. 66.
40. Stefansson, 1929, p. 288.
41. Lee, 1967a, p. 26.
42. ———, 1967a, pp. 36–39.
43. Collins, 1940, p. 560.
44. ———, 1940, pp. 563–65.
45. ———, 1940, p. 566.
46. Birket-Smith, 1929, 2, p. 14.
47. Collins, 1940, pp. 264–65;
    Giddings, 1967, p. 100.
48. Collins, 1940, p. 560.
49. Fournier, 1970.

CHAPTER 9

1. Lee, 1967c.
2. Mowat, 1965.
3. Rieth, pp. 169–74.
4. Holand, 1940, pp. 78–79.
5. Clarke and Erskine, 1961;
   Spjeldnaes and Henningsmoen, 1963.
6. Bird, 1945, pp. 179–81.

7. Mallery, pp. 60–61, 171–75.
8. Ingstad, 1969.
9. Pohl, 1966, Chap. 15;
   ———, 1972.
10. Means, pp. 292–304;
    Mongé and Landsverk, pp. 127–30;
    Mallery, pp. 182–90.

11. Pohl, 1966, pp. 201–2.
12. ———, 1966, pp. 197–201;
    Mongé and Landsverk, Chaps.
    8, 12.
13. Godfrey, 1955.
14. Hovgaard, pp. 259–77.
15. Sherwin, 1940–53.
16. Howley, pp. 16–18.
17. Beck, p. 20.
18. ———, p. 41.
19. Mallery, pp. 138–55.
20. Holand, 1940, pp. 264–86;
    Curran, pp. 144–56.
21. Holand, 1940, pp. 244–51.
22. ———, 1940, p. 248.
23. Curran, pp. 175–84, 211–34.
24. Elliott, 1941.
25. Curran, pp. 30–34;
    Holand, 1946, pp. 178–210.
26. Mongé and Landsverk, Chaps.
    19, 20.
27. Breckenridge, 1955.
28. Mongé and Landsverk, pp. 202–
    6.
29. Mongé and Landsverk, p. 206.
30. Stefansson, 1938, 2, p. 23.
31. ———, 1938, 1, p. 126.
32. ———, 1938, 1, p. 125.
33. ———, 1938, 2, p. 56.
34. ———, 1938, 2, p. 56.
35. ———, 1938, 1, p. 86.
36. ———, 1938, 1, p. cxv.
37. Markham, pp. 6–7.
38. ———, p. 8.
39. ———, p. 17.
40. ———, p. 18.
41. ———, p. 23.
42. ———, p. 41.
43. ———, p. 20.
44. de Rochefort, C., *Historie Nat-
    urelle et Morale des Iles An-
    tilles de l'Amerique,* Rotterdam,
    1658, pp. 194–95.
45. Curran, p. 155.
46. Melko, 1969.
47. Dunbar, 1952.
48. Gini, 1958.
49. Ingstad, 1966, Chap. 31.

Bibliography

Adam, Paul, "Étude Nautique du Problème du Vinland," *Révue d'Histoire Économique et Sociale*, Vol. 37 (Paris, 1959), pp. 20–42.

———— "Il n'y a pas de Mystère du Vinland," *Inter-Nord*, No. 9 (Paris, École des Hautes Études de la Sorbonne, March 1967), pp. 239–56.

Andersson, Theodore, *The Problem of Icelandic Saga Origins* (New Haven and London, Yale University Press, 1964).

Anthropologica, continuing series (Ottawa, University of Ottawa, since 1955).

The Arctic Pilot, 3 volumes (London, British Admiralty Hydrographic Office, 1915).

Babcock, William H., "Early Norse Visits to North America," *Smithsonian Miscellaneous Collections*, Vol. 59 n. 19 (Washington, 1913).

———— "Recent History and Present Status of the Vinland Problem," *Geographical Review*, Vol. 11 (New York, American Geographical Society, 1921), pp. 265–82.

Bagrow, L., and Skelton, R. A., *History of Cartography* (Cambridge, Harvard University Press, 1964).

Beamish, N. L., *The Discovery of America by the Northmen* (London, T. & W. Boone, 1841).

Beazley, C. R., *The Dawn of Modern Geography* (Oxford, Clarendon Press, 1896–1906; New York, P. Smith, 1949).

Beck, Horace P., *Gluskap the Liar and Other Indian Tales* (Freeport, Me., B. Wheelright Co., 1966).

Bekker-Nielsen, H. and Olsen, T. D., *Bibliography of Old Norse-Icelandic Studies, 1966* (Copenhagen, Munksgaard, 1967).

Bird, Junius, "Archaeology of the Hopedale Area, Labrador," *American Museum of Natural History, Anthropological Papers,* Vol. 39 (New York, 1945), pp. 121–186.

—— "Conservation Work at the L'Anse au Meadow, Newfoundland, Archaeological Site," *National Geographic Society Research Reports for 1964* (Washington, 1969), pp. 21–25.

Birket-Smith, Kai, *Caribou Eskimos,* 2 volumes (Copenhagen, Gyldendal, 1929).

—— *Anthropological Observations on the Central Eskimos* (Copenhagen, Gyldendal, 1940).

Boas, Franz, *The Central Eskimo* (Washington, U. S. Bureau of American Ethnology, 1888; Lincoln, University of Nebraska Press, 1964).

Boland, Charles M., *They All Discovered America* (Garden City, Doubleday & Company, Inc., 1961).

Breckenridge, R. W., "Norse Halbreds," *American Anthropologist,* Vol. 57 (Menasha, 1955), pp. 129–31.

Brögger, Anton W., *Winlandfahrten* (Hamburg, 1939).

—— and Shetelig, H., *The Viking Ships* (Oslo, Dreyers forlag, 1951).

Brondsted, Johannes, "Problemet om Nordboer i Nordamerika for Columbus" (English summary pp. 123–52), *Aarboger for Nordish Oldkyndighed ok Historie, 1950* (Copenhagen, 1951), pp. 1–152.

Brown, Lloyd, *The Story of Maps* (New York, 1949).

Brunn, Daniel, "The Icelandic Colonization of Greenland," *Meddelelser om Grönland,* Vol. 57 (Copenhagen, Reitzel, 1918).

Canadian Hydrographic Service, *Atlantic Coast Tide and Current Tables,* 1966 ed. (Ottawa, 1966).

Canadian Weekly Bulletin, continuing series of Department of External Affairs (Ottawa).

Carpenter, Rhys, *Behond the Pillars of Hercules* (New York, Delacorte, 1966).

Carus-Wilson, E. M., "The Overseas Trade of Bristol," *Bristol Record Society's Publications,* Vol. 7 (Bristol, 1937).

Cassidy, Vincent H., *The Sea Around Them* (Baton Rouge, Louisiana State University Press, 1968).

Cavalli-Sforza, Luigi, "Genetic Drift in an Italian Population," *Scientific American* (New York, August 1969), pp. 30–37.

Christensen, T. P., *The Discovery and Re-Discovery of America* (Cedar Rapids, 1934).

Clarke, A. H. and Erskine, J. S., "Pre-Columbian Littorina Littorea in Nova Scotia," *Science*, Vol. 134 (Washington, American Association for Advancement of Science, 1961), pp. 293–94.

Collins, H. B., "Outline of Eskimo Prehistory," *Smithsonian Miscellaneous Collections*, Vol. 100 (Washington, 1940).

———— "The L'Anse aux Meadows Archaeological Site in Northern Newfoundland," *National Geographic Society Research Reports for 1961–62* (Washington, 1970), pp. 39–49.

Colvin, Ian, *The Germans in England* (London, "National Review" Office, 1915).

Conference on the Climate of the Eleventh and Sixteenth Centuries, *Proceedings*, (Boulder, Colorado, 1962).

Cooper, Paul Fenimore, Jr., "The Representation of Greenland on the Vinland Map," *Proceedings of the Vinland Map Conference*, ed., Wilcomb Washburn (Chicago, Chicago University Press, 1971).

Crone, G. R., *The Discovery of America* (London, Hamilton, 1969).

Curran, James Watson, *Here Was Vinland* (Sault St. Marie, *Sault Daily Star*, 1939).

Currelly, C. T., "Viking Weapons Found near Beardmore, Ontario," *Canadian Historical Review* (March 1939).

Dansgaard, W., *et al*, "One Thousand Centuries of Climatic Record from Camp Century on the Greenland Ice Sheet," *Science*, Vol. 166 (Washington, American Association for Advancement of Science, 1969), pp. 377–81.

De Costa, B. F., *The Pre-Columbian Discovery of America by the Northmen* (Albany, J. Munsell, 1868).

———— *Columbus and the Geographers of the North* (Hartford, M. H. Mallory, 1872).

Degerböl, M., "Animal Bones from the Norse Ruins at Brattahlid," Appendix 1 of "Brattahlid," *Meddelelser om Grönland*, Vol. 88 (Copenhagen, Reitzel, 1934).

———— "Animal Remains from the West Settlement in Greenland," *Meddelelser om Grönland*, Vol. 88 (Copenhagen, Reitzel, 1936).

Diringer, David, *The Alphabet* (New York, Philosophical Library, 1948; London, Hutchinson, 1968).

Donworth, Albert B., *Why Columbus Sailed* (New York, Exposition Press, 1953).

Drinnan, R. H. and Prior, L., "Physical Characteristics of the Ungava Bay Area," *Geographical Bulletin*, No. 7 (Ottawa, Department of Mines and Surveys, 1955), pp. 17–37.

Dunbar, M. J., "The Ungava Bay Problem," *Arctic*, Vol. 5 (Ottawa, Arctic Institute of North America, 1952), pp. 4–16.

Durand, Dana, *The Vienna-Klosterneuberg Map Corpus*, (Leiden, E. J. Brill, 1952).

Elliott, O. C., "The Case of the Beardmore Relics," *Canadian Historical Review*, Vol. 22 (Toronto, University of Toronto Press, 1941), pp. 254–79.

Fernald, M. L., "Notes on the Plants of Wineland the Good," *Rhodora*, Vol. 12 (Boston and Providence, New England Botanical Club, 1910), pp. 17–38.

———— "The Natural History of Ancient Vinland and its Geographical Significance," *American Geographical Society Bulletin*, Vol. 47 (New York, 1915), pp. 686–87.

Fischer-Møller, Knud, *Skeletal Remains of the Central Eskimos* (Copenhagen, Gyldendal, 1937).

———— "The Medieval Norse Settlements in Greenland," *Meddelelser om Grönland*, Vol. 89 (Copenhagen, Reitzel, 1942).

Fiske, John, *The Discovery of America*, 2 Volumes (Boston and New York, Houghton-Mifflin, 1892).

Flaherty, Robert J., "Two Traverses across Ungava Peninsula, Labrador," *Geographical Review*, Vol. 6 (New York, American Geographical Society, 1918), pp. 116–32.

Flandrau, Grace, "The Verendrye (1685–1743) Expeditions in Quest of the Pacific" *Oregon Historical Society*, Vol. 26 (June 1925).

Fossum, Andrew, *The Norse Discovery of America* (Minneapolis, 1918).

Foucault, Michel, *The Order of Things* (New York, 1970).

Fournier, Jean, "In Canada's Far North, the Boom Has Just Begun," *Reference Papers*, No. 126 (Ottawa, Canadian Department of External Affairs, 1970).

Fried, Jacob, "A Survey of the Aboriginal Populations of Quebec and Labrador," *Eastern Canadian Anthropological Series*, No. 1 (Montreal, McGill University Press, 1955).

Gad, Finn, *History of Greenland* (London, Hurst, 1970).

Gade, John A., *The Hanseatic Control of Norwegian Commerce During the Late Middle Ages* (Leiden, E. J. Brill, 1951).

Gathorne-Hardy, G. M., *The Norse Discoverers of America* (Oxford, Clarendon, 1921).

———— "A New Theory on the Wineland Voyages," *Geographical Journal*, Vol. 66 (London, Royal Geographical Society, 1925), pp. 53–57.

Geographical Journal, continuing series of Royal Geographical Society, London.

Geographical Review, continuing series of American Geographical Society; formerly A.G.S. *Bulletin* and A.G.S. *Journal,* New York.

Giddings, James L., *Ancient Men of the Arctic* (New York, Alfred A. Knopf, Inc., 1967).

Gini, Corrado, "On the Extinction of the Norse Settlements in Greenland," *Papers from the Institute of Economics of the Norwegian School of Economics and Business Administration,* No. 10 (Bergen, 1958).

—— "The Location of Vinland," *Papers of the Institute of Economics of the Norwegian School of Economics and Business Administration,* No. 13 (Bergen, 1960).

Godfrey, William S., "Vikings in America: Theories and Evidence," *American Anthropologist,* Vol. 57 (Menasha, 1955), pp. 35–43.

Goldstein, Thomas, "Geography in Fifteenth Century Flornece," *Merchants and Scholars,* ed., J. Parker (Minneapolis, University of Minnesota Press, 1965), pp. 9–32.

—— "Conceptual Patterns Underlying the Vinland Map," *Renaissance News,* Vol. 19, No. 4 (New York, Renaissance Society of America), pp. 321–31.

Goodwin, William B., *The Truth about Leif Eiriksson* (Boston, Meador, 1941).

—— *The Ruins of Great Ireland in New England* (Boston, Meador, 1946).

Gordon, Cyrus, *Before Columbus* (New York, Crown, 1971).

Gray, Edward F., *Leif Eiriksson* (New York, Oxford University Press, 1930).

Greely, A. W., "The Origin of Stefansson's Blonde Eskimo," *National Geographic Magazine* (December, 1912).

Grenfell, Wilfred T., *Labrador, the Country and the People* (New York, The Macmillan Company, 1913).

Grönlands Historiske Mindesmaerker, 3 Volumes (Copenhagen, K. Nordiske Oldskrift-selskab, 1845).

Guthmundsson, Barthi, *The Origin of the Icelanders* (Lincoln, University of Nebraska Press, 1967).

Hallberg, Peter, *The Icelandic Saga* (Lincoln, University of Nebraska Press, 1962).

Hapgood, Charles H., *Maps of the Ancient Sea Kings* (Philadelphia and Toronto, Chilton, 1966).

Harp, Elmer, Jr., "Cultural Affinities of the Newfoundland Dorset

Eskimo," *National Museum of Canada Bulletin*, No. 200 (Ottawa, 1964).

Haugen, Einar, *Voyages to Vinland* (New York, Alfred A. Knopf, Inc., 1942).

Hermannsson, Halldór, *The Problem of Wineland* (Ithaca, Cornell University Press, 1936).

—— *The Vinland Sagas* (Ithaca, Cornell University Press, 1944).

Holand, Hjalmar R., *Westward from Vinland* (New York, Duell, Sloan & Pearce, 1940).

—— *America: 1355–1364* (New York, Duell, Sloan & Pearce, 1946).

—— *Explorations in America before Columbus* (New York, 1956).

Holborn, Hajo, "The History of Ideas," *American Historical Review*, Vol. 73 (Washington, American Historical Society, 1968), pp. 683–95.

Holtved, Erik, "Archaeological Investigations in the Thule District," *Meddelelser om Grönland*, Vol. 141 (Copenhagen, Reitzel, 1944).

Honti, John T., "Late Vinland Tradition (The Thorbjörn Narrative)," *Modern Language Quarterly*, Vol. 1 (Seattle, University of Washington Press, 1940), pp. 339–55.

Hovgaard, William, *The Voyages of the Norsemen to America* (New York, American-Scandinavian Foundation, 1914).

Howley, James, *The Beothuks or Red Indians* (Cambridge, Cambridge University Press, 1915).

Ingstad, Helge, *Land Under the Pole Star* (New York, St. Martins, 1966).

—— *Westward to Vinland* (New York, St. Martins, 1969).

Isachsen, Gunnar, "Découverte de vestiges nordiques dans l'archipel polaire Américain," *Terre-Air-Mer* (*La Géographie*), Vol. 10 (Paris, Masson, 1904), pp. 371–76.

—— "Nordboernes faerder til Norderseta," *Det Norske Geografiske Selskabs Aarbog*, Vol. 18 (Christiana, 1907), pp. 20–32.

Isachsen and Isachsen, "Hvor Langt Mot Nord Kom De Norrøne Grønlendinger På Sine Fangstferder I Ubygdene?" *Norske Geografisk Tidsskrift*, Vol. 4.

Islandica, continuing annual series, (Ithaca, Cornell University Press, since 1908).

Jenness, Diamond, "The Life of the Copper Eskimos," *Report of the Canadian Arctic Expedition*, Vol. 12 (Ottawa, National Museum of Canada, 1922).

—— "Physical Characteristics of the Copper Eskimos," *Report of the Canadian Arctic Expedition,* Vol. 12, Pt. B (Ottawa, National Museum of Canada, 1923).

——— "A Bio-Bibliography of Diamond Jenness by Asen Balekci," *Anthropologica,* Vol. 4 (Ottawa, University of Ottawa Press, 1957), pp. 37–46.

Johanesson, Jon, "The Date of the Composition of the Saga of the Greenlanders," *Saga Book of the Viking Society,* Vol. 16 (London, 1962–65), pp. 54–66.

Jones, Gwyn, *The Norse Atlantic Saga* (London and New York, Oxford University Press, 1964).

——— *A History of the Vikings* (New York and London, Oxford University Press, 1968).

Jones, Howard M., *O Strange New World* (New York, The Viking Press, Inc., 1964).

Jones, Marcus E., *Astragalus* (Salt Lake City, privately published, 1923).

Kaups, Matti, "Shifting Vinland—Tradition and Myth," *Terrae Incognitae,* Vol. 2 (Amsterdam, N. Israel, 1970), pp. 29–60.

——— "Shifting Vinland—Tradition and Myth: A Rejoinder," *Terrae Incognitae,* Vol. 3 (Amsterdam, N. Israel, 1971), pp. 97–105.

Kelsall, John P., *The Migratory Barren-Ground Caribou of Canada* (Ottawa, 1968).

Kendrick, Thomas D., *A History of the Vikings* (New York, Charles Scribner's Sons, 1930; Barnes & Noble, Inc., 1968).

Kimble, George H. T., *Geography in the Middle Ages* (London, Methuen, 1938; New York, Russell & Russell, 1968).

——— *Geography of the Northlands* (New York, American Geographical Society, 1955).

Krogh, Knud, *Viking Greenland* (Copenhagen, Danish National Museum, 1967).

The Labrador and Hudson Bay Pilot, 2nd Ed. (Ottawa).

Ladurie, Emmanuel LeRoy, *Times of Feast, Times of Famine* (Garden City, Doubleday & Company, Inc., 1971).

Lamb, H. H., *The Changing Climate* (London, Methuen, 1966).

Larsen, Sofus, *The Discovery of North America Twenty Years Before Columbus* (Copenhagen and London, Levin & Munksgaard, 1925).

Las Casas, Bartolomé, *Historia de las Indias* (Madrid, M. Ginesta, 1875).

Lattimore, Owen, "Chingis Khan and the Mongol Conquest," *Scientific American* (August, 1963), pp. 54–68.

Lee, Thomas E., "The Norse in Ungava," *Anthropological Journal of*

Canada, Vol. 4 No. 2 (Ottawa, Anthropological Association of Canada, 1966), pp. 51–54.

———— "Archaeological Investigations, Deception Bay, Ungava Peninsula, 1965," *Anthropological Journal of Canada,* Vol. 5 No. 3 (Ottawa, Anthropological Association of Canada, 1967), pp. 14–39.

———— "A Summary of Norse Evidence in Ungava, 1968," *Anthropological Journal of Canada,* Vol. 5 No. 3 (Ottawa, Anthropological Association of Canada, 1967), pp. 41–48.

———— "Ancient European Settlement Revealed at Payne Lake, Ungava, 1965," *Travaux Divers,* No. 16 (Quebec, Laval University Centre d'Études Nordiques, 1967), pp. 28–116.

———— "A Summary of Norse Evidence in Ungava, 1968," *Anthropological Journal of Canada,* Vol. 6 No. 4 (Ottawa, Anthropological Association of Canada, 1968), pp. 17–21.

———— "Archaeological Discoveries, Payne Bay Region, Ungava, 1966," *Travaux Divers,* No. 20 (Quebec, Laval University Centre d'Études Nordiques, 1968).

———— "Archaeological Findings, Gyrfalcon to Eider Islands, Ungava 1968," *Travaux Divers,* No. 27 (Quebec, Laval University Centre d'Études Nordiques, 1969).

Levin, Maksim G., *Physical Anthropology and Ethnogenic Problems of the Peoples of the Far East* (Toronto, University of Toronto Press, 1963).

Liestol, Knut, *The Origins of the Icelandic Family Sagas* (Oslo, Instituttet for sammenlignende kulturforskning, 1930).

Lucas, H. S., "Medieval Economic Relations between Flanders and Greenland," *Speculum,* Vol. 12 (Cambridge, Medieval Academy of America, 1937), pp. 167–81.

Magnusson, Magnus and Palsson, Herman, *The Vinland Sagas* (New York, New York University Press, 1966).

Mallery, Arlington H., *Lost America* (Columbus and Washington, 1951).

Marcus, G. J., "The Greenland Trade Route," *Economic History Review,* Series 2 Vol. 7 (London, Economic History Society, 1954).

Markham, Albert H., *The Voyages and Works of John Davis* (London, 1880).

Mathiassen, Therkel, *Archaeology of the Central Eskimos,* 2 Volumes (Copenhagen, Gyldendal, 1927).

———— "Norse Ruins in Labrador," *American Anthropologist,* Vol. 30 (Menasha, 1928), pp. 569–79.

——— "Inugsuk, A Medieval Eskimo Settlement," *Meddelelser om Grönland*, Vol. 77 (Copenhagen, Reitzel, 1931), pp. 145–340.

——— "The Eskimo Archaeology of the Julianehaab District," *Meddelelser om Grönland*, Vol. 118 (Copenhagen, Reitzel, 1936).

Maycock, Paul F., "Plant Records of the Ungava Peninsula, New to Quebec," *Canadian Journal of Botany*, Vol. 41 (Ottawa, National Research Council, 1963), pp. 1277–79.

McGill University Geography Department, "Report on the Physical Environment of Southern Baffin Island," *Rand Corporation Memorandum RM-2362-1-PR* (Santa Monica, 1963).

Means, Philip A., *The Newport Tower* (New York, H. Holt & Co., Inc., 1942).

Meddelelser om Grönland, continuing series with many articles in English (Copenhagen, Reitzel).

Meldgaard, Jorgen, "The Dorset Culture," *Kuml* (Aarhus, 1955), pp. 173–77.

Melko, Matthew, "The Interaction of Civilizations," *Journal of World History*, Vol. 11 (Neuchatel, 1969), pp. 559–77.

Merrill, William S., "The Vinland Problem Through Four Centuries," *Catholic Historical Review*, Vol. 21 (Baltimore, Catholic University of America, 1935), pp. 21–48.

Mongé, Alf, and Landsverk, Ole G., *Norse Medieval Cryptography in Runic Carvings* (Glendale, Norseman Press, 1967).

Morison, Samuel E., *Admiral of the Ocean Sea* (Boston, Little, Brown and Company, 1942).

——— "It All Boils Down to What We Knew Before," *New York Times Book Review* (New York, November 7, 1965), pp. 7, 92.

——— *The European Discovery of America: The Northern Voyages* (New York, Oxford University Press, 1971).

Moss, Edward L., *Shores of the Polar Sea* (London, Marcus Ward, 1878).

Mowat, Farley, *Westviking* (Boston and Toronto, Little, Brown and Company, 1965).

——— *Canada North* (Boston and Toronto, Little, Brown and Company, 1967).

——— *The Polar Passion* (Boston and Toronto, Little, Brown and Company, 1967).

Mulroy, Martin J., *The Irish in America* (Boston, Angel Guardian Press, 1906).

Naess, Almar, *Hvor la Vinland?* (English summary pp. 241–46) (Oslo, 195?).

Nansen, Fridtjof, *In Northern Mists*, 2 Volumes (London, Heinemann, 1911).

—— "The Norsemen in America" (with panel discussion), *Geographical Journal*, Vol. 38 (London, Royal Geographical Society, 1911), pp. 557–80.

Nares, George, *Narrative of a Voyage to the Polar Sea*, 2 Volumes (London, S. Low-Marston-Searle & Rivington, 1878).

Neatby, Leslie H., *In Quest of the Northwest Passage* (London, Constable, 1958).

—— *Conquest of the Last Frontier* (Athens, Ohio University Press, 1966).

Noice, H., "Further Discussion of the 'Blond' Eskimos," *American Anthropologist*, Vol. 24 (1922).

Nörlund, P., "Buried Norsemen at Herjolfsnes," *Meddelelser om Grönland*, Vol. 67 (Copenhagen, Reitzel, 1924).

"The Norse Discovery of America: A Compilation in Extenso of all the Sagas, Manuscripts and Inscriptive Memorials relating to the Finding and Settlement," *Norroene Society Anglo-Saxon Classics*, Vol. 15 (1907).

Nowosad, F. S., "Farming in the Sub-Arctic," *Agricultural Institute Review*, Vol. 14 No. 1 (Ottawa, 1959), pp. 11–14, 53.

Nunn, George E., *The Geographical Conceptions of Columbus* (New York, American Geographical Society, 1924).

O'Gorman, Edmundo, *The Invention of America* (Bloomington, Indiana University Press, 1961).

Oleson, Trygvie, *Early Voyages* (Toronto, McClelland & Stewart, 1963).

O'Neill, J. J., "The Geology of the Arctic Coast of Canada West of Kent Peninsula," *Report of the Canadian Arctic Expedition*, Vol. 11 (Ottawa, Canadian National Museum, 1924).

Oxenstierna, Eric, *The Norsemen* (Greenwich, Connecticut, New York Graphic Society, 1965).

—— "The Vikings," *Scientific American* (May 1967).

Parry, John Horace, *The Age of Reconnaissance* (Cleveland, World Publishing; London, Weidenfeld & Nicolson, 1963).

Patch, H. R., *The Other World* (Cambridge, Harvard University Press, 1950).

Piggott, S., *Ancient Europe* (Chicago, Aldine; Edinburgh, Edinburgh University Press, 1965).

Pohl, Frederick J., *The Lost Discovery* (New York, W. W. Norton & Company, Inc., 1952).

———— *Atlantic Crossings before Columbus* (New York, W. W. Norton & Company, Inc., 1961).

———— *The Viking Explorers* (New York, Thomas Y. Crowell, 1966).

———— *The Viking Settlements of North America* (New York, Clarkson N. Potter, 1972).

Polunin, Nicholas, "Botany of the Canadian Eastern Arctic," 4 Volumes, *Bulletin* (Biological Series) (Ottawa, National Museum of Canada, 1940–48).

Porsild, A. E., "Plant Life in the Arctic," *Canadian Geographical Journal*, Vol. 42 (B) (Ottawa, 1951), pp. 120–45.

———— "Illustrated Flora of the Canadian Arctic Archipelago," *National Museum of Canada Bulletin*, No. 146 (Ottawa, 1957).

Power, Eileen, ed., *English Trade in the Fifteenth Century* (London, Routledge, 1933; New York, Barnes & Noble, Inc., 1966).

Quimby, George I., "The Old Copper Culture and the Copper Eskimos, an Hypothesis," *Arctic Institute of North America Technical Papers*, No. 11 (Montreal, 1962), pp. 76–79.

Quinn, David B., "The Argument for the English Discovery of America between 1480 and 1494," *Geographical Journal*, Vol. 127 (London, Royal Geographical Society, 1961), pp. 277–85.

Rafn, Carl C., *America Discovered in the Tenth Century* (New York, Jackson, 1838).

———— *Antiquités Americaines* (Copenhagen, Royal Society of Northern Antiquities, 1845).

Ramskou, Thorkild, *Vikingernes Hverdag/Everyday Viking Life* (Danish/English parallel texts) (Copenhagen, 1967).

Rasmussen, Knud, *The Netsilik Eskimos* (Copenhagen, Gyldendal, 1931).

Reeves, Arthur, *The Finding of Wineland the Good* (London, H. Frowde, 1895; New York, B. Franklin, 1967).

Reman, Edward, *The Norse Discoveries and Explorations in America* (Berkeley and Los Angeles, University of California Press, 1949).

Rieth, Adolf, *Archaeological Fakes* (London, Barrie & Jenkins, 1970).

Rousseau, Jacques, "Les Zones Biologiques de la Peninsula Quebec-Labrador et l'Hemiarctique," *Canadian Journal of Botany*, Vol. 30 (Ottawa, National Research Council, 1952), pp. 463–74.

Roussell, A., "Sandnes and the Neighbouring Farms," *Meddelelser om Grönland*, Vol. 88 (Copenhagen, Reitzel, 1936).

———— "Farms and Churches in the Medieval Norse Settlements of Greenland," *Meddelelser om Grönland*, Vol. 89 (Copenhagen, Reitzel, 1941).

Rudenko, S. I., *The Ancient Culture of the Bering Sea and the Eskimo Problem* (Toronto, University of Toronto Press, 1961).

Saga Book, continuing series of the Viking Society for Northern Research, London.

Sanz, Carlos, *La Ciencia Moderna ¿Consecuencia Directa del Des-
cubrimiento de America?* (Madrid, Real Sociedad Geografica,
1971).

Sauer, Carl O., *Northern Mists* (Berkeley and Los Angeles, University
of California Press, 1968).

Scandinavia Past and Present, Vol. 1 (Copenhagen, Edvard Hen-
riksen, 1959).

Scisco, L. D., "The Tradition of Hvitramannaland," *American Historical Magazine* (New York, Publishing Society of New York,
1908), pp. 379–88, 515–24.

Seymour, Maurice C., *Mandeville's Travels* (New York and London,
Oxford University Press, 1967).

Sherwin, Reider T., *The Viking and the Red Man,* 7 Volumes (New
York and London, Funk & Wagnalls, 1940, 1942; Bronxville,
1944–53).

Simmons, Herman G., "Eskemåernas Utbredning och Vandringsvägar,"
Ymer, Vol. 25 (Stockholm, 1905), pp. 190–91.

Simpson, Jacqueline, *Everyday Life in the Viking Age* (London, Bats-
ford; New York, G. P. Putnam's Sons, 1967).

Skelton, Raleigh A., *et al, The Vinland Map and the Tartar Relation*
(New Haven and London, Yale University Press, 1965).

Small, Alan, "Historical Geography of the Norse Viking Colonization
of the Scottish Highlands," *Norsk Geografisk Tidsskrift,* Vol. 22
(1968), pp. 1–16.

Soper, J. Dewey, "Solitude of the Arctic," *Canadian Geographical
Journal,* Vol. 7 (Montreal, 1933).

Spjeldnaes, N. and Henningsmoen, K. E., "Littorina Littorea: An
Indicator of Norse Settlement in North America?" *Science,* Vol.
141 (Washington, American Association for Advancement of Science, 1963), pp. 275–76.

Steensby, Hans P., *The Norsemen's Route from Greenland to Wineland* (Copenhagen, Koppels, 1918).

Stefansson, Vilhjalmur, "The Stefansson-Anderson Expedition," *Anthropological Papers of the American Museum of Natural History,* Vol. 14 (New York, 1914).

———— *The Friendly Arctic* (New York, The Macmillan Company,
1921; 1943).

———— *My Life with the Eskimos* (New York, The Macmillan Company, 1929).

———— *The Three Voyages of Martin Frobisher*, 2 Volumes (London, Argonaut, 1938).

———— *Unsolved Mysteries of the Arctic* (New York, The Macmillan Company, 1939).

———— *Ultima Thule* (New York, The Macmillan Company, 1940).

———— *Greenland* (Garden City, Doubleday & Company, Inc., 1942).

Storm, Gustav, *Monumenta Historica Norvegiae* (Christiana, A. W. Brøgger, 1880).

———— "Studies on the Vinland Voyages" (English translation), *Memoires de la Société Royale des Antiquaires du Nord* (Copenhagen, 1888), pp. 307–70.

Stover, Robert, *The Nature of Historical Thinking*, (Chapel Hill, University of North Carolina Press, 1967).

Sturlason, Snorre, "The Heimskringla: A History of the Norse Kings," *Norroene Society Anglo-Saxon Classics*, Vols. 7–9, (1907–11).

Sullivan, L., "The Blonde Eskimos—A Question of Method," *American Anthropologist*, Vol. 24 (Menasha, 1922).

Sveinsson, Einar, *Dating the Icelandic Sagas* (London, Viking Society for Northern Research, 1958).

Swanton, John R., "The Wineland Voyages," *Smithsonian Miscellaneous Collections*, Vol. 107 No. 12 (81 pp.) (Washington, 1947).

Tanner, Väinö, *Newfoundland-Labrador*, 2 Volumes (Cambridge, Cambridge University Press, 1947).

Taylor, Eve G., "A Letter Dated 1577 from Mercator to John Dee," *Imago Mundi*, Vol. 13 (Stockholm, Kartografisk Sällskapst, 1956), pp. 56–68.

Taylor, William E., "Review and Assessment of the Dorset Problem," *Anthropologica, New Series*, Vol. 1 (Ottawa, Canadian Research Center for Anthropology, 1959), pp. 24–46.

———— "A Cape Dorset Culture Site on the West Coast of Ungava Bay—Archaeology," *National Museum of Canada Bulletin*, No. 167 (Ottawa, 1960).

Thompson, Michael Welman, *Novgorod the Great* (New York, Praeger; London, Evelyn-Adams & Macay, 1967).

Thomson, James Oliver, *History of Ancient Geography* (Cambridge, Cambridge University Press, 1948).

Thordarson, Matthias, *The Vinland Voyages* (New York, American Geographical Society, 1930).

Thule Expedition (fifth), *Report*, 11 Volumes (published at various places and times).

Tikhomirov, B. A., "The Treelessness of the Tundra," *Polar Record*, Vol. 11, No. 70 (Cambridge, Scott Polar Research Institute, January 1962).

Torfaeus, Thormod, *History of Ancient Vinland* (New York, U. S. Catholic Historical Society Press, 1891).

Tornöe, J. K., *Columbus in the Arctic* (Oslo, Bokcentralen, 1965), pp. 1–93; *Addendum* (Oslo, 1967), pp. 94–131.

United States Air Force, *Operational Navigation Chart*, Nos. C-12, D-15 (1965).

U. S. Navy Hydrographic Bureau, *Arctic Ice and its Drift into the North Atlantic Ocean* (Washington, May 1947).

Vebaek, C. L., "Ten Years of Topographical and Archaeological Investigations in the Medieval Norse Settlements in Greenland," *Proceedings of the 32nd International Congress of Americanists* (Copenhagen, 1956), pp. 732–43.

Verhoog, P., *De Ontdekking van Amerika voor Columbus* (Hilversum, C. de Boer jr., 1958).

Vignaud, Henry, *Toscanelli and Columbus* (London, Sands, 1902).

The Viking (London, Watts, 1966).

Wahlgren, Erik, "Further Remarks on Vínland," *Scandinavian Studies*, Vol. 40 (Menasha, February 1968), pp. 26–35.

Washburn, Wilcomb, "The Meaning of 'Discover' in the Fifteenth and Sixteenth Century," *American Historical Review*, Vol. 68 (October 1962), pp. 1–21.

Weeks, L. J., "Cumberland Sound Area, Baffin Island," *Canada Department of Mines Geological Survey, Summary Report*, Part C (1927).

Williamson, James Alexander, *The Cabot Voyages and Bristol Discovery under Henry VII* (Cambridge, Cambridge University Press, 1962).

Wise, Jennings, *The Mystery of Columbus* (Charlottesville, Virginia, Monticello, 1946).

Wolfe, Michel, "Norse Archaeology in Greenland since World War II," *American Scandinavian Review*, Vol. 49 (New York, American Scandinavian Foundation, 1961), pp. 380–392.

Wood, Casey A. and Fyfe, F. Marjorie, *The Art of Falconry of Frederick II* (Stanford, Stanford University Press; London, H. Milford, 1943).

Index

Adam, Paul, 54
Adam of Bremen, 47, 75, 173
  on Norse dependence on cattle,
    33
  on Vinland as Wineland, 29–31
Africa
  Norse knowledge of, 172–73
  Vinland placed in, 109, 173
Agriculture. See Farming
Alaska
  Lapland mistaken for, 79–85
  Norse maps of, 74
    15th-century, 89–90
  Norsemen in, 91, 92, 143–44
  Thule Eskimo migration from, 76–
    77
    back-wave of migration, 141–44
    limits of, 97
    maps indicating reverse path of,
      87, 91
Alcoholic beverages, Norse, 31
  the Church and, 36
Aldrin, Edwin E., Jr., 100
Alexander, Gerard L., Foreword by,
    vii–ix
Alexander III (Pope), 177
Alexander VI (Pope), 107
Algonkin Indians teach white man
    Lacrosse, 152

Algonkin language, Norse words in,
    152
America. See Alaska; Archaeological
    excavations; Canada; Colum-
    bus, Christopher; Maps; Vin-
    land
American dream, origin of, 29
Amundsen, Roald, 91
Analytical techniques, archaeologi-
    cal, 69–70
Andersson, Theodore, 12n
Animals
  cattle, 22, 33–34, 131
  North American, in Norse trade,
    85, 127, 130, 150, 178–79
  sheep, 10, 64
Annals of Iceland, 74
Archaeological excavations
  of central Arctic, 129–30, 134
  deciding on putting off, 69–70
  as decisive, 66–67
  of Great Lakes, 156–57
  of L'Anse au Meadows, 13, 14,
    177
  of medieval European village in
    caribou grazing area, 150
  Norse-Indian relations and, 153–
    54

Norse penetrations into interior of
America and, 154–55
of Norse presence in northlands,
116–17
of Norsemen among Eskimos, 117–
20
techniques for, 69–71
Thorvald Eiriksson's grave and,
67–68
Arctic
central
archaeological excavations of,
129–30, 134
cairns in, 135
copper of, 134–35
Eskimos and Norse dispersal
into, 131–35
Lancaster Sound as only usable
portal to, 129
maps of, 129–30, 141–43
"forest islands" of, 19–26
Norse maps of Canadian arctic
coast, 74–75
sub-arctic summer dews, 55
tree line and, 20
vegetation of eastern Canadian,
52–54
Arctic Archipelago, Norse maps of,
74–75, 86
Arctic Pilot, 58, 59, 65
"Arctic prairies," 53–54
Arctic willows, 25
Arimphians, myth of, 80–81
Armstrong, Neil, 100
Artifacts, 117–21, 156–57. *See also*
Archaeological excavations
Asgard, gods of, 7
Asia
American continents misconstrued
as east coast of, 102, 103
Americas explored from, 167–68
and Columbus' sailing time for
reaching America, 106, 170
Greenland as off the coast of, 103–
4
new information displaced from

Scandinavia to northeast corner of maps of (15th cen-
tury), 105
Norse discoveries associated with
(1250), 104
practical possibility of voyage to
(15th century), 101, 106
Atlantic winds and currents, 107–8
Aztec civilization, 108

Baffin Island
characteristics of, 16–17
gold sought in, 95, 158
Helluland placed on, 12, 14–19,
24, 51
mapped, 87
map involving Smaller Misun-
derstanding, 127–28
Norse maps of, 74–75
Markland and, *see* Markland
trees in south-central, 21
Vinland as part of, 50–51; *see
also* Vinland
Baltic Sea frozen over during little
Ice Age, 130
Bardsson, Ivar, 87–88, 122, 131, 132,
147
Beardmore find, 156
Beothuk Indians, 153
Beyer, Absalon Pedersson, 178
Bible, long *i* in translation of, 31
Bird, Junius, 151
"Blond" Eskimos, 136–38
Brandan, Saint, Irish myth of, 46–47
Bremen, Adam von. *See* Adam of
Bremen
Bristol (England), slave trade and,
96–97
Columbus and, 107, 174

Cabbage, wild, 40, 41
Cabot, John, 96–97, 106
Cairns
in central Arctic, 135
as landmarks in Iceland, 126–27

Norse, 117–18, 121
  described, 124, 126–27
  Scotland and, 135
Canada
  Norse dispersal into, 129–45
  Norse maps of, 74–75, 151
  Thule Eskimo migration across
    northern, 76. *See also* Thule
    Eskimos—migration of
  vegetation of eastern Canadian
    arctic, 52–54
  Vinland placed in, *see* Vinland
Carbon dating, 68–70
Caribou
  annual cycle of migration of, 149–
    50
  Eastern and Western settlements'
    trade in, 149–50
  Norse dispersal and, 131–33
  Tunit legend and hunting of, 138–
    39
Cartography. *See* Maps
Cassidy, Vincent H., 104
Catalan map (1380), 104
Catholic church. *See* Roman Catho-
    lic Church
Cattle, Norse, 22, 33–34, 131
Celts, as "Westmen," 1
Chidley, Cape (Canada), 23
Chidley Islands, Cape (Canada),
    described, 58–59
Chidley Peninsula, Cape, 51, 52
China, size of earth and contradic-
    tion involving sailing from
    Scandinavia to, 104
Christianity. *See* Roman Catholic
    Church
Chromatographic analyzer, gas, 69
Church, excavated, 122
Cibes (Latin), meaning of, 37
Civilizations
  Aztec and Mayan, 108
  birth of, 168
  remains of Norse, around Great
    Lakes, 155

Clavus, Claudius, 89–91, 103–5, 116,
    143, 144
Cloth, woven, as treasure, 118
Cnoyen, Jacob, 36, 37, 40, 104
Columbus, Christopher, vii, 99–113
  African coast known to, 173
  discovery of America by
    cost of voyage, 101
  cult of Columbus and, 99–100,
    112–13
  downward revision of size of de-
    gree and, 106
  earth as pear-shaped and, 171–
    72
  earth's sphericity and, 169–71
  foreknowledge available to,
    106–7, 169–70
  Grand Misunderstanding made
    acceptable by, 110
  Indians and diplomacy of, 152
  meeting of two worlds and, 166,
    169
  motivation for voyage, 101–3,
    109
  Norse explorations as spark for,
    73–74, 109–10
  Roman Catholic Church and,
    179–80
  success predetermined, 112–13
  sureness of, 179–82
  travels prior to, 173–74
  white men preceding him to
    Caribbean, 108
  Iceland visited by (1477), 106–7,
    173–74
  slavery and, 107, 174
Computers, archaeological uses of,
    69
Coopering, 119
Copper
  of central Arctic, 134–35
  Eskimo uses of, 158–59, 161
Copper Eskimos, 134–35, 159
"Cordware Culture" people, 2
Cortesão (scholar), 109
Crete, 168

Crocke (Dutch), meaning of, 37
Crowberry wine, 31
Crusader tax, Greenland pays, 176, 178
Cumberland Peninsula (Baffin Island), Helluland as, 12, 14–19, 24, 51
Cyprus, 168

Dairy farming. *See* Farming
Davis, John, 160–61
Davis Strait, 17, 18
Day, John, 107
Denmark, 111
Denmark Strait, 18
Determinism, Columbus' glorification and philosophical, 112–13
Devil Island (Canada), 126
Dews, summer sub-arctic, 55
Diana Bay (Canada), 53
Discoveries, as "in the air" of the epoch, 100. *See also* Columbus, Christopher; Eiriksson, Leif
Donworth, Albert, 106
Dorset Eskimos, 76n
culture of, 120–21
as legendary Tunit, 139
Duason, Jon, 129
Ducier, Dominicus, 105, 109
Dutch (language), 36, 37

Early Voyages (Oleson), 129
Earth
as pear-shaped, 171–72
size of
contradiction involving Scandinavia-China sailing and, 104
downward revision of, 105–6
sphericity of
belief in, 101
Columbus' sailing directions and, 169–71
Middle Ages and problem of, 82–83
Spanish monarchs and, 180

Earthly paradise, Middle Ages and, 46
Eastern Settlement (at modern Julianehaab, Greenland), 17, 85
area revisited (1578), 159–60
dependence upon hunting in, 147–48
Eskimos and
contacts, 142
trade, 148
See also Eskimos
Indians and emigration of, 153
lack of traces of Norsemen in (1721), 162–63
last European contacts with, 164
Little Ice Age and climatic deterioration in, 130–31
pirates and, *see* Pirates
post-Columbian white man influx to America and dispersal of, 153–54
Ruin Island artifacts and artifacts of, 121
Western Settlement and
cut off from each other, 130–33
effect of loss of agriculture on both, 147–49
estrangement between them, 147
trade with dispersed Western Settlement, 148–50
Western Settlement contact with Thule Eskimos and, 88
Egede, Hans, 93, 162–63
Egede, Niels, 93
Egypt, 168
Eider houses, 124–26, 141
Einarsson, Björn, 147
Eirik the Red (Eirik Thorvaldsson Rauda), xv–xvi, 175
banished, 8
colonizes Greenland, 8–9
Hauksbok version of saga of, 19
naming of Greenland by, 30
pastureland and, 33

Thorhall the Hunter and, 43, 44,
61–62
vin and upbringing of, 42
Eiriksdottir, Freydis, 12, 67
Eiriksson, Leif, vii, xvi, 43, 169
expeditions of, 11–12, 24, 27
Columbus vs. Eiriksson in discovery of America, 99
cutting hay and timber and, 34,
35, 47
Helluland, *see* Helluland
Markland, *see* Markland
priests carried on, 175
vegetation and, 31
houses of
archaeological excavations and,
68–71
built, 61–64, 67
location of, 51–52
Thorvald Eiriksson and, 57–58
location of Vinland and, 66
archaeological evidence and, 67,
68
sub-arctic dew and, 55
vin and upbringing of, 42
Vinland named, 53
Eiriksson, Thorstein, 12, 43, 68
Eiriksson, Thorvald, expeditions of,
12, 52
death of, 58–59, 67
grave of, 67–68
Leif's house and, 57–58
Ellesmere Island, mapping, 87
England claims Newfoundland, 111–
12. *See also* Pirates; Slavery
Erlendsson, Hauk, 21. *See also*
Hauksbok
Eskimo folk tales
of Norsemen, 74, 123
of pirates, 93–94
Eskimo ruins excavated in Labrador,
151
Eskimo trade chain, 116, 117, 121
"Eskimopolis," 125–26
Eskimos
"Blond," 136–38

Copper, 134–35, 159
copper used by, 158–59, 161
Haneragmiut, 136
Inugsuk, *see* Inugsuk culture
Thule, *see* Thule Eskimos
Etruscan alphabet, 5–6
Euclid, 100
Eurasia, maps of North America dis-
placed into maps of, 74
European village, excavation of
medieval, 150
Europeans, genes of, among Eski-
mos, 136–37. *See also* Maps
Excavations. *See* Archaeological ex-
cavations

Falconry, 85
gyrfalcons and, 85, 127, 130, 179
Family history
Norse legacy to European "Age of
Discovery" and sagas as, 73
reciting, 6–7
recording, in writing, 7–8
Farming, Norse dairy, 10
effects of loss on Eastern and
Western settlements, 147–49
onset of Little Ice Age and, 130–
32
survival habits and, 88, 90–91
Ferdinand V (King of Spain), 101,
102, 180
Feuds, Norse, 3, 4, 8
Finmark, 26
Finnbogi, 67
Firearms, Norse, 93n
Fireplaces, Eskimo uses of Norse,
123, 124, 126
Fisher-Möller, Knud, 135
Flaherty, Robert, 21
Florida, 181
Folk story identifying New World
as Old World, 81–82. *See also*
Eskimo folk tales
Follins Pond (Mass.), Norse dry
dock at, 151, 154
"Forest islands," Arctic, 19–26

Fossum, Andrew, 12n
Fox "tower traps," 140–41
Frederick II (Holy Roman Emperor), 85
Freydis. See Eiriksdottir
Frobisher, Sir Martin, 16, 95, 158–60, 162
Frobisher Bay (Canada), 16
Frobisher Peninsula (Canada), 16, 27

Geit, Halli, 82
Geographia Universalis, 36
Geography of the Northern Lands (Adam von Bremen), 173
Glaciers in Little Ice Age, 130
Gnupsson, Bishop Eirik, 67, 71, 85, 175–76
Godthaab (Greenland), 11. See also Western Settlement
Gold associated with west instead of the east (15th century), 108–9
Gold-hunting voyages, 95, 158
Gordon, Cyrus, 2n
Grand Misunderstanding, defined, 79
Grapes, location of Vinland and, 34–48
Gray, Edward, 25
Great Lakes
    Norse artifacts from, 156–57
    Norse civilization remains in, 155
Great Teutonic Migration, 2–3
Greenland, xvi, xvii
    as off Asian coast, 103–4
    Bjarni Herjolfsson circumnavigates, 18–19
    claim to new lands and, 111
    colonized, 8–10
    dairy farming and, 10
        effects of loss, 147–49
        onset of Little Ice Age and, 130–32
        survival habits and, 88, 90–91
    disappearance of Norsemen and, 162–64
        theories accounting for, 163–64
    explorations based on, 11–12
        penetration into interior of America, 154–58
        southern limit of explorations, 151–54
        first modern glimpse of (1576–78), 158–59
    forest of, 21
    geographic features of, 9–10
    intermixing of races in, 135–36
    map making and, 75; see also Maps
    named, 30
    Norse movement north on coast of, 117
    people of, 30
    placement of
        in doubt, 103, 104
        spread of Norsemen over North America and, 104–5
    political death of medieval, 112
    "rediscovery" of, 93
    Roman Catholic Church and, 175–79
        alcoholic beverages and, 36
        Catholic priests living in Greenland, 175–76
        conversion of Norsemen, 7
        Crusader tax paid, 176, 178
        deserting the Church, 91, 111–12
        isolated from rest of Catholic world, 177
        loss of Greenland colonies and, 179
        reconversion of Norsemen, 93
        Thule Eskimo-Norsemen contact and, 87, 91
    settlements of
        changes in survival habits, 88, 90–91
        disappearance of, 77

dispersal and changes in culture, 133–34

European knowledge of Norse activities, 108, 174

growth of, 85

pirate attacks on, 78–79, 88–90, 93–97, 124; *see also* Pirates

ruins of, 10–11

See also Eastern Settlement; Western Settlement

sheep grazing on, 64

Thule Eskimos migration to, *see* Thule Eskimos

trade between Europe and, 85–86

ceases, 92

Tunit dialect as dialect of, 140

word *vin* and, 32, 42

Gregorius (Pope), 177–78

Grenfell, Wilfred, 61

Groc (Dutch), meaning of, 36, 37

Grocland, 36, 37, 39, 40

Gyrfalcons, white, 85, 127, 130, 179

Hall, Charles C., 95

Hall Peninsula (Baffin Island), 25

Hand, European custom of kissing, 160

Haneragmiut Eskimos, 136

Harald Fairhair (first king of Norway), 4

Hauksbok, 32, 33. *See also* Erlendsson

Haven, Cape (Baffin Island), 27, 50

Hay, 34–35, 47

Headlands of Markland, 22, 23

Helgi, 67

Helluland (Slatestoneland)

barrenness of, 21

location of, 12, 14–19, 24, 51

Herjolfsson, Bjarni, 11, 15–19, 24

Heyerdahl, Thor, 165–82

Historiography favoring Roman over Teutonic influence, 110

History

family

Norse legacy to European "Age

of Discovery" and sagas as, 73

reciting, 6–7

recording (in writing), 7–8

of ideas, 100

oral

effect of written history on, 7–8

facts preserved through, 5, 6, 95

recorded on parchment, 86

political motivation and teaching of, 110–11

Holand, Hjalmar, 157

Holtved, Erik, 119–21

Horsford, Eben, 99

Houses

eider, 124–26, 141

of "Eskimopolis," 125–26

of Karlsefni, 67

Leif Eiriksson's house and, 51, 52

of L'Anse au Meadows, 13, 14, 177

of Leif Eiriksson

archaeological excavation and, 68–71

built, 61–64, 67

location of, 51–52

Thorvald Eiriksson and, 57–58

Norse adoption of Eskimo building methods, 122–23

Pamiok Island, 70, 71

rectangular, 120–21

Eskimo uses of, 123, 124

trees for, 19–20, 24, 25

Hovgaard, William, 32, 63

Hudson Strait, 51, 59

Humanism, 105

Hunting

Eastern Settlement dependence on, 147–48

Norse adoption of Eskimo techniques, 122

Norse shift to, 90, 91

Tunit legend and, 138–39

in Western Settlement, 131–34

Hvitramannaland, 13–14

Hybrid willows of the Arctic, 25

Iceland
   cairns as landmarks in, 126–27
   clock time and, 57
   Columbus visit to (1477), 106–7,
      173–74
   converted to Christianity, 7
   discovery of
      Celtic, 1
      Norse, 1–2, 4
   forests of, 25
   highest peak of, 5
   illegal trade with (15th century),
      97
   modern inhabitants of, 2
   outlaws as original settlers of, 8n
   word vin and, 32, 42, 48
Icelandic (language), Old Norse
   and, 33
Icelandic maps, earliest known, 75
Ideas, history of, discovery of
   America and, 100
India, 170–72, 181
Indians
   Beothuk, 153
   Cuban, assert presence of pre-
      Columbian white men, 108
   emigration of Eastern Settlement
      and, 153
   Eskimo relations with, 158–59
   Kensington rune stone and, 155–
      56
   Norse knattleikr game and, 152
   Norse relations with, 152–54, 162
      hostile tribes and, 151, 152
   Spaniards and, 166–67
Ingstad, Helge, 13, 32, 83, 93, 95,
   126n, 151, 163, 177
"Insel Colci," 40
"Insula Dicolzi," 39, 40
Insulae Fortunatae, 46
Inugsuk culture, 118–21, 128, 160
   disappearance of, 163–64

   disappearance of Norsemen and,
      162
   migration back wave and, 143
Inugsuk island (Greenland), 117–18
Inventio Fortunatae, 96
Irish
   Hvitramannaland, 13–14
   Iceland discovered by, 1
   myth of St. Brandan, 46–47
Iron
   Eskimo uses of, 159–61
   spectral test of tools of, 120
Iroquois Indians, 153
Isabella I (Queen of Spain), 101,
   102, 180
Isachsen, Gunnar, 126

Jenness, Diamond, 135, 137, 140,
   141
John XXI (Pope), 178
Jones, Gwyn, 12, 54
Julianehaab (Greenland), 11. See
   also Eastern Settlement

Karlsefni, Thorfinn (The Valiant),
   expeditions of, 12, 14, 47, 178
   houses of, 67
   Leif's house and, 51, 52
   livestock and, 33–34
   Markland and, 26–27
   misidentification of New World
      with Old World and, 84–85
   natives encountered, 21–22, 75
   Thorhall the Hunter and, 44
   trading, 77, 118
   unsuccessful attempt to colonize
      Vinland, 59–64
   vegetation and, 31, 32
   vin and, 43
Karlsefni's Saga, 12. See also Saga
   of Eirik the Red
Kayak, Norse adoption of, 122
Kensington rune stone, 155–56
Kingigtorssuaq island (Greenland),
   117
Kissing. See Hand

Kitsorsauq island (Greenland), 118
Kjalarnes (Ness of the Keel), named, 52, 58
Klengenberg, 136
Knattleikr (game), 152
Krakke (Flemish), meaning of, 37
Krok (Dutch), meaning of, 37
Krossanes (Ness of the Cross), named, 59

Labrador
  Eiriksson voyage and, 51
  Eskimo ruins excavated in, 151
  Markland placed in, 19–20, 26
  Labrador & Hudson Bay Pilot, 60, 63
Lacrosse (game), 152
La Hontan, Baron de (Louis Armand de Lom d'Arce), 161–62
Lancaster Sound, as only usable portal to central Arctic, 129
Landsverk, Ole, 157
L'Anse au Meadows (Newfoundland), 13, 14, 177
Lapland, Alaska mistaken for, 79–85
Lapps, 80
Las Casas, Bartolomé, 108, 180
Latin alphabet adapted to Old Norse language, 7
La Vérendrye, Sieur de (Pierre Gaultier de Varennes), 156
Law, Norse, 4, 6
Leaf Bay, Lief's house and, 52
Leaf Lake (Canada), as Vinland, 56, 57
Legends of Tunit, 138–39. *See also* Eskimo folk tales; Folk story; Myths
Lee, Thomas E., 68, 70, 71, 141, 150
Leif the Lucky. *See* Eiriksson, Leif
Levin, Maksim, 137
Literature, lack of written Norse, 5
Little Ice Age, 90, 130–32
Livingstone, David, 137

Locoweed, 39

Magellan, Ferdinand, 170
Magnetic compass, 97–98, 150
Magnusson, Magnus, 12
Mallery, Arlington H., 151, 153
Mandan Indians, genetic remnants of Norsemen in, 156
Mandeville, John, 82
Maps, 73–98
  of Alaska, 74
    15th-century map, 89–90
  appearance of Quebec-Labrador Peninsula on European, 149, 150, 155, 157
  of Arctic Archipelago, 74–75, 86
  of Asia, *see* Asia
  of Baffin Island, 87
    map involving smaller Misunderstanding, 127–28
    Norse maps of, 74–75
  of Canada, 74–75, 151
  of central Arctic
    Norse origin of, 129–30, 141
    Thule Eskimo origin of, 141–43
  Columbus voyage and pre-Columbian, 102–3
  earth and, *see* Earth
  gold associated with west instead of east on, 108
  Grand Misunderstanding on, 79
  Icelandic, 75
  identifying New World as Old World, 74, 77–81
  identifying North American land in 15th-century European, 104–6
  introducing new lands in western ocean, 109
  magnetic compass and, 97–98, 150
  Norse knowledge in post-Columbian, 112
  pirate transmission of, 92–95
  of Scandinavia, *see* Scandinavia; Thule Eskimo
  Alaskan maps, 79

hard-copy maps, 77
incorporated into north of Old
    World, 77
as map makers, 75, 77
Norse vs. Eskimo origin of, 157–
    58
Norsemen learn concepts of,
    91–92, 115, 128
Marcellus (German bishop), 179
Markland
    location of, 12, 14–15, 19–27, 51
    Old Norse words in connection
        with wood and, 25–26
    Quebec vs. Baffin Island as, 23–
        24
    sands and, 26–28
    wood cover as landmark, 22–23
    location of Vinland and, 55
    1347 voyage to, 67
Marsson, Ari, 14
Mass spectrometer, 69
Matheus (German bishop), 179
Mathiassen, Therkel, 117–19, 121,
    128
Maya Indians, 168
Mayan civilization, 108
Mela (geographer), 80
Memorization of all learned informa-
    tion, 5, 6
Mercator, 36–37
Merrill, William S., 12n
Mesopotamia, 168
Mexico, 167
Migration
    of caribou, 149–50
    Great Teutonic, 2–3
    Norse, 2–3
    Thule Eskimo, 76–77
        back-wave of, 141–44
        limits of, 97
        maps indicating reverse path,
            87, 91
Misunderstanding. See Folk story;
    Grand Misunderstanding;
    Maps; Smaller Misunderstand-
    ing

Mongols, as Arimphians, 80, 81
Morison, Samuel E., 100
Mowat, Farley, 71, 150
Muntzer, Hieronoymus, 106
Musmanno, Michael, 99
Myths
    of Arimphians, 80–81
    mythical Riphean Mountains, 80
    of St. Brandan, 46–47
    See also Eskimo folk tales; Folk
        story; Legends

Nachvak Fiord, described, 62–63
Nansen, Fridtjof, 32, 33, 46, 47, 163
Nansen theory, 136
Navigational ability
    of Christian nations, 4
    of Norsemen, 4–5
Neutron activation, 69
Newfoundland
    British claim to, 111–12
    Norse-Indian relations in, 152–53
    Norse ruins in northern, 151
Newport Tower (R.I.), 151, 154
Newton, Sir Isaac, 100, 101
Nicholas V (Pope), 88, 93, 96, 174,
    179
Nipigon, Lake (Canada), 156, 157
Norse Atlantic Saga, 54
Norse cairns, 117–18, 121
    described, 124, 126–27
Norse time, clock time and, 57
North Atlantic, Columbus voyage
    and true distance across, 106
Northwest Passage, sailing through,
    91
Norway
    claim to new lands and, 111, 175
    European communication with
        Greenland by way of, 97
    first king of, 4
    Greenland trade as royal monop-
        oly of, 92
    Mediterranean world's contact
        with, 174–76

slavery and treaty of 1432 between England and, 96
Vinland exploration and, 165–66
Nova Scotia, 150–52
Nuclear magnetic resonance spectrometry, 69

Oklahoma, Norse rune stones in, 151
Olav, Saint (King of Norway), 175
Oleson, Trygvie, 129, 141
Olmec Indians, 168–69
Oral history
effect of written history on, 7–8
facts preserved through, 5, 6, 95
recorded on parchment, 86

Palestine, 168
Palsson, Herman, 12
Pamiok Island excavations, 70, 71
Paper, absence of, among Norsemen, 5
Parchment, 5–7
Pastureland
Eirik the Red and, 33
Vinland as, 30–48
Payne Basin, as Vinland, 56, 57
Payne Bay (Canada)
excavations at, 70
L. Eiriksson's house and, 52
vegetation of, 52–53
Permafrost, excavation and, 117
Philosophical determinism, glorification of Columbus and, 112–13
Pirates
disappearance of Norsemen and, 163
Eskimo folk tales of, 93–94
map transmission by, 92–95
raids by, 78–79, 88–90, 93–97, 174
Planifolia willows, 25
Plants, classification of, in Middle Ages, 40
Pohl, Frederick J., 30
Polar bears, trade in, 85, 130
Political motivation, teaching history and, 110–11

Polo, Marco, 104, 106, 108, 172
Polunin, Nicholas, 39, 52–53, 66
Portugal, 107–8
Private property, importance of, to Norsemen, 3, 4
Psalter map, 80
Ptolemy, 105, 106, 171

Quebec (Canada), as location of Markland, 23–24
Vinland, 51–71
Quebec/Labrador Peninsula, Norse-Indian relations and, 152
Quetzalcoatl, 167–69
Quinn, David, 107

Rape (hybrid of wild cabbage and turnip), 40, 41
Rasmussen, Knud, 140
Ravens used in navigation, 5
Reactionaries, Vikings as, 33
Reeves, Arthur, 12n
Reman, Edward, 51, 54
Renaissance, pagan Norse vitality as key factor in, 110
Riphean Mountains, mythical, 80
Roman Catholic Church
clock time introduced to Iceland by, 57
Columbus and, 179–80
Greenland and, 175–79
alcoholic beverages and, 36
Catholic priests living in Greenland, 175–76
conversion of Norsemen, 7
Crusader tax paid, 176, 178
deserting the Church, 91, 111–12
isolated from rest of Catholic world, 177
loss of Greenland colonies and, 179
reconversion of Norsemen, 93
Thule Eskimo-Norsemen contact and, 87, 91
Roman Empire, 45

Romans, writing as invention of, 6
Ross, Sir James Clark, 17
Ruin Island (Greenland), 121
Rune stones
  Kensington, 155–56
  in Oklahoma, 151
Runic alphabet, 5–6
Russia, "Cordware Culture" people in, 2
Ruysch, Johann, 37, 81

Saemund the Learned, 7
Saga, defined, 6. *See also* History; *Tale of the Greenlanders*
Saga of Eirik the Red, 12, 31, 38, 51, 59
Sailing directions
  Columbus', 169–71
  memorized, 5
Sails, Eskimo uses of, 159
Sands of Markland, 26–28
Sandwort (wild grain), 38
Sauer, Carl, 14
Scalping, 153
Scandinavia
  earth's size and sailing to China from, 104
  mapped, 75, 77
  misidentification of Thule Eskimos and, 79–80
  new information displaced from, to northeast corner of maps of Asia (15th century), 105
  New World maps mistaken for maps of, 83–87, 103
  Norse migration to, 2
  as remote, for medieval scholars, 78
"Schleswig Turkey," 150
Schliemann, Heinrich, 95
Scotland, cairns and, 135
"Secondary climatic optimum," 23
Self-deception, as Middle Ages art, 45–46
  still present, 113
Seven Islands Bay, 60

Seward Peninsula (Alaska), 89
Sheep, 10, 64
Sherwin, Reider T., 152
Ships, abandoning, 133, 134
Sigurd Jordsalfarer (Sigurd Pilgrim-to-the-Holy-Land, King of Norway), 173, 176
Simmons, Herman, 125–26
Slavery, 93–97
  Bristol involved in, 96–97
  Columbus and, 107, 174
  British-Norwegian treaty of 1432 and, 96
  Norse disappearance and non-Christian qualification for, 163
  Smaller Misunderstanding defined, 83–84
  See also Pirates
Snail shells excavated in Nova Scotia, 150–51
Soper, Dewey, 21
South America, mistaken for Africa, 109
Spain
  Columbus and, 179, 180
  Indians and, 166–67
  New World and, 166–67
Spectral tests of iron tools, 120
Spectrometry, 69
Stanley, Henry, 137
Stapp (scientist), 100
Stefansson, Vilhjalmur, 54, 107, 140, 141, 160, 163
  "Blond" Eskimos and, 136–37
Survival of the fittest among the Norsemen, 3–4
Sverre (King of Norway), 31
Syria, 168

Tahuglauk people, 162
Tale of the Greenlanders, 12, 15, 26, 34, 38, 47, 65–66
Tanner, V., 53, 55
Tasiuyak Arm, described, 62–63
Thloyde, John, 106
Thorhall the Hunter, 38, 39

abandons expedition, 44–45
characteristics of, 43–44
Eirik the Red and, 43, 44, 61–62
Karlsefni expedition and, 61–62, 64
Lief's house and, 52
Thule culture
disappearance of, 162–64
as fusion of Dorset Eskimos and Norsemen, 129n
most recent examples of, 141–42
Norse culture amalgamated with, 118–28
Norse dispersal into central Arctic and, 135
Thule Eskimos
absorb Norsemen, 135–38
berries collected by, 54
caribou herds and, 132
Christianity of Norsemen and, 87, 91
contact with Norsemen, 87–88, 122–24, 142
contact re-established, 86, 91
Eastern Settlement and contact of Western Settlement with, 88
first contact, 75–76, 117, 119
hostility and, 152
ongoing contacts (16th and 17th centuries), 158–63
copper and, 134, 158–59, 161
desire to agree with white man's theories, 83
Dorset culture and, 120–21, 139
European genes among, 136–37
fireplaces used by, 123, 124, 126
folk tales of pirates, 93–94
interdependent relationship of Norsemen with, 115–16
as map makers, 75, 77
Alaskan maps, 79
hard-copy maps, 77
incorporated into North of Old World, 77

Norse vs. Eskimo origin of, 157–58
Norsemen learn concepts of, 91–92, 115, 128
migration of, 76–77
back-wave of, 141–44
limits of, 97
maps indicating reverse path of, 87, 91
misidentification of, 79–85
Norse adopt Eskimo ways, 132–33
Norse dispersal into central Arctic and, 131–35
"tower traps" and, 140–41
trade between Norsemen and, 117–19, 122, 127, 148
as Tunit, 138–40
Vinland's location and, 75, 76
Toltec Indians, 168–69
Toolmaking, 119, 120
Tools, excavated, 118–20
Torfaeus, 57
Torngat Mountains, 61, 65
Toscanelli, Paolo, 106, 107
"Tower traps," fox, 140–41
Trade
of Eastern and Western settlements, 148–50
Eskimo-Norsemen, 117–19, 122, 127, 148
Europe-Greenland, 85–86
ceases, 92
illegal, with Iceland (15th century), 97
by Karlsefni, 77, 118
in North American animals, 85, 127, 130, 150, 178–79
as Norwegian royal monopoly, 92
slave, see Slavery
Trade chain, Eskimo, 116, 117, 121
Tree line, Arctic and, 20, 50
Trees, Markland's location and, 19–26
Trinkets, 118–20, 123–24
Tsukernik, David, 107
Tundra, tree growth and, 20

Tunes, Nicholas, 161
Tunit legend, 138–40
Tyrkir the German, 34, 35, 38–39

Ungava Bay (Canada), 23, 53–66
  excavations at, 70
  Karlsefni misses entrance to, 59
  post-Vinland sagas referring to,
    150
  vegetation along, 53–54
  Vinland and, 51–52; see also Vin-
    land
  west coast of, 56

Valkendorf, Bishop Erik, 178
Value system of Norsemen, 3–4
Verendrye stone, 156
Vetch (legumous fodder), 37–41
  intoxicating species of, 38–39
  rape and, 40
Vienna-Klosterneuberg map, 39–40
Vignaud, Henry, 107
Viking, meaning of term, 3, 177
Vinland
  as in Africa, 109, 173
  Church and, 175–76
  Columbus and location of, 173–75
  discovery of, vii, 12
  lack of permanent settlements in,
    73
  L'Anse au Meadows as, 13, 14,
    177
  last record of Norse travel to, 84,
    85
  location of, vii–viii, xvi, xvii, 49–71
    exact spot, 57
    on Baffin Island, 50–51
    Thule Eskimos and, 75, 76
  meaning of word, 12, 28–48
  natives of, fear cattle, 22
  Norway and explorations of, 165–
    66
  recording oral sagas and, 86
  trees of, 24
Vinland Map. See Yale Vinland Map
Vinland sagas, 12

Vinum (Latin), vin (Old Norse)
  and, 41–43
Virga, Albertin de, 108
Virginia, 151
Von Braun, Werner, 100

Walford, Naomi, 44
Walsperger map, 39–40
Washington Irving Island, 124
Weapons, excavated, 118–20
Weeks, L. J., 24
West Indies, 109
Western Settlement (at modern
    Godthaab, Greenland), 17, 85
  area revisited (1585–87, 1656),
    160, 161
  dispersal of, 148, 149, 153
  Eastern Settlement and
    cut off from each other, 130–33
    effect of loss of agriculture on
      both, 147–49
    estrangement between them, 147
    trade with dispersed Western
      Settlement, 148–50
    Western Settlement contact with
      Thule Eskimos and, 88
  farming conditions deteriorate on,
    130–32
  hunting and dispersal of, 131–34
  lack of traces of Norsemen in
    (1721), 162–63
  last European contacts with, 164
  Little Ice Age and climatic de-
    terioration in, 130–32
  seeking ways around Baffin Island,
    127
  Thule Eskimos and, see Thule
    Eskimos
"Westmen," 1
Wine, making and drinking, 31
Wine-land, clock time and, 57
Wineland, Vinland as, 30–48
Wise, Jennings, 108
Wissler, Clark, 138

Wood (timber)
   gathering of, from Vinland, 34–36
   location of Markland and, 19–26
      wood cover as landmark and,
      22–23
   Old Norse word in connection
     with, 25–26

Yale Vinland Map, xvi, 36, 37, 74

Zeitz map, 40
Zeno, Niccolò, 88, 108, 118, 122,
   148